MANAGING MULTIPLE BOSSES

MANAGING MULTIPLE BOSSES

How to Juggle Priorities, Personalities & Projects —and Make It Look Easy

Pat Nickerson

AMACOM

American Management Association

New York • Atlanta • Boston • Chicago • Kansas City • San Francisco • Washington, D.C.
Brussels • Mexico City • Tokyo • Toronto

Library of Congress Cataloging-in-Publication Data

Nickerson, Pat.
    *Managing multiple bosses : how to juggle priorities, personalities
& projects—and make it look easy / Pat Nickerson.*
      p. cm.
    Includes index.
    ISBN 0-8144-7025-4
    1. Management. 2. Decision making. I. Title.
HD31.N4898   1998
650.1—dc21   *98–29095*
                                                   CIP

Printing number

10   9   8   7   6   5   4   3   2   1

Contents

List of Cases

Acknowledgments

To the executives, managers, administrative assistants, military personnel, government officials, teachers, and nurses whose stories and suggestions helped form this book.

To my husband and partner of many years, Ken Nickerson, whose logistical and business skills free me to write a book now and then. And for the thousand gifts of the spirit he lavishes on our life together.

To my training and consulting colleague, Dr. Deborah Smith-Hemphill, whose partnership in our company's work enriches and extends each experiment we launch.

To longtime friend Pat Walsh, for sharing her executive experiences at two universities, one public utility, and several Peace Corps installations and for her insights on solutions for nonprofits and global organizations.

To Mary Ellyn Wyatt, for her careful reading of the manuscript and helpful suggestions based on her years in business and government.

To Andrea Iadanza, AMA project manager, whose client-centered dedication enlivens the many courses we teach for her audiences.

To Jacqueline Flynn of AMACOM for her steadying judgment, positive suggestions, and upbeat help in preparing this book.

Introduction

Do you manage production? Lead an accounting group? Head up engineering projects? Design software? Manage administration for a top executive team? Sell or service products or systems? Manage distribution? Maintain a facility? Whether you must beat the clock or race the calendar—you feel the pressure of serving many masters and their legitimate, competing demands.

- You wish you could put more time in your day.
- You juggle tasks and hope you won't bobble the ball.
- You strive for quality and service, despite tighter deadlines.
- You struggle to excel for customers, clients, colleagues, and bosses, but you worry about burnout.

This interactive book should help you rev up without flaming out. Take heart! If your work pressures appear beyond remedy, you'll find plenty of sympathy among your colleagues in this book, and you'll get fresh answers from peers as well as from experts—answers you can apply right away.

Today, when you ask business and government colleagues if they report to multiple bosses, you get a spirited yes more often than not. In this era of team and matrix management, a single performer may lead one project, serve on another, and consult for a third, fourth, or fifth. In healthy organizations, you view everyone as a customer: Internal or external—they are all "your boss." Most likely, you have set up electronic linkages with many internal and some external customers and clients. Because linkage is instant, they expect service to be instant as well. They may ignore your need for time to decide or latitude to negotiate. The pressure is definitely on! If you learned to accept these realities early—if you accustomed yourself gradually to multitasking—you may feel armed, technically and emotionally, to manage your multi-boss traffic with aplomb. However, if you've been resisting, denying, or delaying acceptance of the multi-boss phenomenon, you may find yourself straining under the pressures and resenting the demands that now outrun you. Whatever level of readiness you've achieved, the ideas and tools in this book are designed to help you accept what you must, negotiate what you can, and gain added skills or easier access to multitasking for many bosses.

While all managers and workers must adjust, administrative assistants and top secretaries find the pressure to change particularly dramatic. For more than a century, the world's top executive secretaries could expect to work for just one boss, the chief executive. But in a 1997 American Management Association (AMA) survey, nearly half the respondents—48 percent of the senior administrative assistants—were found to have four or more bosses. Only 22 percent had a single boss, even at the top. In many organizations, the assistant is sole aide to the CEO, CFO, COO, and CIO! While this gives the top assistant enviable insights into the management process, it also adds head-spinning conflicts to very long workdays. Because of the ingenuity they employ, executive assistants offer cases and solutions that earn a prominent place in this book. Whatever your job, you'll glean useful ideas from the many practical cases and solutions proffered by these assistants.

Why This Multi-Boss Phenomenon?

Reengineering and Downsizing

Globally, companies and bureaucracies keep trimming down. They've eliminated management layers without eliminating workloads. With fewer levels handling more work, each survivor carries heavier burdens. Companies say that automation will bridge the chasm. While computer speed and capacity certainly help with high-volume tasks, they also swell the torrent of useless data pouring into our lives.

New Software

Accounting, scheduling, drafting, and project coordination tasks—once done manually by mid-level accountants, engineers, and administrators—are now run more economically by assistants and technicians with smarter software. Companies reap cost reductions (calculations do go faster), but the communication pace heats up to 150 or more e-mails per day, per manager. In many nonemergency functions, workers now warn correspondents that they will review e-mail only once or twice daily; otherwise, deadline work suffers.

Contact Expectations

If you are a senior manager or technologist, you once relied on call-screening to protect your time. But now customers use e-mail, fax, and voice mail to access you directly. Therefore, you must limit caller expectations by using precise outgoing messages to buy time or refer traffic elsewhere. Mostly, your callers demand instant, personal responses to even the most complex questions. Many people will phone you to see if an e-mail has reached you. Their real purpose: To jump the queue and get "me first" service. Should they expect your answers to flow as fast as their questions? Have you lost the right to do research or to deliberate over difficult matters?

Global Competition

Ivory towers are emptied: Even the most senior managers are shooed out the door to chase new business worldwide. With a laptop in every briefcase, and a cell phone at every ear, business travelers can never escape work. They must make new deals on the fly, relying on thinner administrative staffs to service and support complex negotiations. Traveling CEOs, engineers, designers, consultants, and salespeople fill every airplane seat, and phone lines are strained to capacity. Can we humans perform as tirelessly as the machines? Should we?

Team Management

On the plus side, technical complexity has forced a welcome blurring of hierarchies. Because advanced projects require such myriad skills, you may be invited to play at high-stakes tables because of your technical, not your political, pull. Matrix management keeps order; early involvement pays off in greater commitment, fewer errors, and shortened project life cycles. At last, rigid lines of authority are broken down; industrial democracy seems within reach. We feel stressed but exhilarated.

Need a Mind-Set Overhaul?

Managing "at the speed of change" has brought challenge, excitement, sleeplessness, and handsome financial rewards to many more managers, assistants, and technicians. But we scarcely have time to enjoy our gains. Vacations are rarer: Extended weekends are all the time we can afford to take. Work–life balance becomes a new Holy Grail.

So for you, regaining your balance may be reason enough to read this book. You are invited to interact with each chapter, noting down your agreements, arguments, and resolves and slowing down to mull over the problems that worry you. You are encouraged to grab new insights and shape new solutions, so you can mount the "work–life merry-go-round" with less dizziness and more delight.

How to Use This Book

Each chapter contains:

- *Briefings:* on the challenges you face as you juggle priorities, personalities, and projects
- *Case problems:* actual dilemmas proposed by seminar members, at public and work site courses, over the past few years
- *First-pass written solutions:* suggestions from seminar members
- *Your reaction:* an invitation to add your opinions
- *Second thoughts:* ideas expressed in seminar group discussions
- *Consensus recommendations:* a synthesis of workable approaches
- *Tool kits:* selected tools and checklists to help you implement solutions
- *Illuminating interviews:* testimonies and survey opinions for added insights
- *Triumphs and turnarounds (or Tragedies):* personal stories from people who got things right or who learned lessons late
- *Summaries:* chapter highlights to help you recall and apply new ideas

Main topics you'll be invited to consider include:

- Communicating under stress
- Preserving priorities
- Saying no to unrealistic demands
- Balancing random tasks against major projects
- Managing stress
- Using assertiveness—or finding something better
- Managing conflicts
- Delegating work when overloaded
- Dealing flexibly with varied personalities
- Handling difficult people—or ordinary people behaving badly— even if that person is you

Though many identities are masked, all questions and answers are real: I've collected them over a period of years as my company trained or consulted for organizations as varied as

American Airlines
Bank of America
Berlex Laboratories
Boston University
Central Maine Power
Exxon
General Electric
Harper Hospital (Detroit)
Hershey Foods
Hewlett-Packard
NASA
Procter & Gamble (Asia)
Professional Secretaries International
Southwest Research Institute
States of Illinois, New York, North Carolina, and Texas
USA Today
U.S. Air Force, Army, and Navy
And hundreds of other organizations that were represented at
    public seminars worldwide.

The answers to our questions were given anonymously, so you'll find them honest and heartfelt. Many issues will resonate with you. You'll find them difficult to solve, case by case. As you proceed, you'll amass a body of convictions that will gradually shape your overall policy for managing your work and career more sanely.

The book closes with final checklists and tools to help you negotiate more mutually satisfying partnerships with your multiple bosses, clients, and colleagues. Work with this book: Interact with it, make it your own. Enjoy it and share it.

If you have a question or a story you want me to know about, contact me through AMA or e-mail me at *nickoftime@compuserve. com.* Dialogue beats monologue every time!

1 Protect Your Priorities

How much of your business week do you spend juggling the demands of bosses, associates, subordinates, and customers? As your workloads multiply, do you get less time to plan? Do you fight fires instead? Do you reach each day's end exhausted, with little to show for it? When we ask these questions at our multiple priorities courses—with nearly 200,000 participants answering so far—we get some interesting contrasts.

How Managers Invest Their Time

Senior executives, director-level and higher, report time usage this way:

30–40 percent:	*Planning* for major risks and opportunities.
20–30 percent:	*Organizing* projects and resources. This effort, both strategic and tactical, involves communicating downward in the organization.
20–30 percent:	*Delegating,* too, involves downward communication.
20–30 percent:	*Communicating* with peers, customers, clients, and the public. Secretaries, sales, and customer service provide a cushion here.
5–15 percent:	*Measuring* is handled mostly by staffers.
3–10 percent:	*Controlling* is handled mostly by staffers also.
2– 5 percent:	*Routines,* such as reading mail, etc., are handled by staffers.

The totals for senior executives can often exceed 150 percent of a normal workweek. Call it overtime, but most entrepreneurs and top managers work eighty- to ninety-hour weeks with pleasure; they consider work as play. Crises get even more dedication.

Mid-level people, customer service, sales, personnel managers, and executive assistants, also work many hours but in a nearly opposite proportion:

5–10 percent:	*Planning.* Compared to their bosses, most middle managers stint on planning. They face so much live action during working hours that they hold planning for after-hours "quiet time." But the clock and their energy tend to run out.
10–30 percent:	*Delegating.* Mid-level people in supervisory or coaching roles spend variable amounts of time teaching tasks to staffers, depending on workers' experience and expertise.
10–30 percent:	*Measuring and Controlling.* Here is true middle management territory. Middle managers are in place to monitor production and control quality and costs.
20–25 percent:	*Handling routines.* Executing authorized work can be important, but draining, when too few helpers available.
40–50 percent:	*Communicating.* This large time expenditure, communicating with peers, senior managers, and customers, seems unavoidable to middle managers and secretaries. They don't quarrel with the amount of time invested, but they worry that so many of these contacts occur randomly, forcing them to cope rather than manage. Logic tells them to invest more in planning, thus preventing future random chaos, but they just can't break free.

You may have noticed that the time totals of mid-level people can also overrun the classic forty-hour workweek (see Figure 1 for a sample time investment chart). Heavy overtime—always a reality for senior people—is now common at every salaried level. Middle managers and administrators in service roles reach the day's end knowing they have assisted many people—including their multiple bosses—but too often, they respond without focus and just barely in time.

Note how the time pyramids in Figure 2 for middle managers are nearly reversed from those of their senior bosses. While technicians and secretaries rush to serve *live* callers and execute scheduled work, they put off the planning, organizing, and delegating that would ensure smoothly flowing work and good coverage for tomorrow. They unwittingly create a climate in which brush fires will break out. They've been forced to invert the management pyramid against their better judgment.

Figure 1. Sample time investment chart.

	Senior Level	Mid-Level
• Plan	30-40%	5-10%
• Organize	20-30	10-20
• Direct/delegate	20-30	10-20
• Measure	5-15	10-15
• Control	3-10	10-15
• Communicate	20-25	40-50
• Perform: Rulebound Work	2-5	20-25
TOTAL	100-155%	100-155%+

Figure 2. Time pyramids.

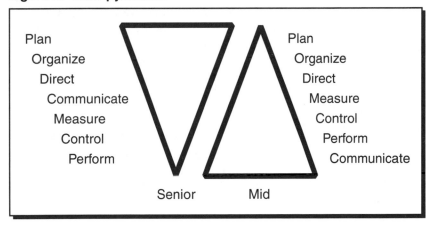

Multi-Bosses, More Clients, and Less Certainty

Today's communication pressures are unique: Urgent messages glut your e-mail, voice mail, and fax twenty-four hours a day. Rarely are you expected to negotiate requests downward. Even the most outlandish demand presents itself as valid, non-negotiable, and urgent!

A decade ago, most workers reported to one boss. If you received a baffling assignment, you knew who to approach for help. Now, with multiple bosses, team and matrix management, and direct and instant links between you and your clients, you face fuzzier lines of authority and far less clarity about who assigned what. You're on your own! You feel the pressure to make progress, across all fronts, without debate. Are you still able to cope? Or do you feel yourself toeing toward the edge of the ledge as your workload crowds you?

Do What Entrepreneurs Do

Wait a minute. Isn't multiple demand the very thing that entrepreneurs relish as they grow a business? An owner learns to address each customer as a number one priority, but owners are never in doubt about which customers really count.

Most business owners have learned an economic reality called *Pareto's Law,* which demonstrates that 20 percent of your effort yields 80 percent of your gain . . . and 20 percent of your customers have the actual or potential power to give you 80 percent of your profits. Apply that to your job: As owner of your career, you must decide which tasks have the potential to produce 80 percent of your value to your company. These select tasks will always get preference when the pressure is on. If—as an owner—you must neglect something (never behaving offensively while doing so), you will downplay the task with less potential to bring either harm or good to the enterprise.

An owner never lets on that he is following Pareto's Law. The small customer is never allowed to feel small. Behind the scenes, an owner scrambles to make enough headway across all fronts to hold all customers. Owners use ingenuity and energy to mask their anxieties while they satisfy and retain all customers. Indeed, most business owners take on more work than they can handle, always seeking more business to stave off a future rainy day. For the smart owner, the top 20 percent of customers will always get the lion's share of attention. Entrepreneurs thrive on little sleep and lots of risk taking. Are you an entrepreneurial worker?

Do you "own" your job? Do you handle multi-boss demands as an entrepreneur would? Which crucial segment of your workload will yield 80 percent of this year's harvest? Focus on your top tier of tasks and clients. Then, develop skill at friendly negotiating with clients one tier down! Find attractions to hold them if they cannot capture a top-priority slot today. When you propose good compromises that retain your second-tier customers, you've built negotiating skill. Use the 20-80 law as the backbone of your validation system. You'll feel more sane and you'll be better able to defend your choices.

Keep Priorities Visible: A Seven-Step Menu

Follow a simple, consistent daily routine to monitor your priorities.

   1. Use a calendar, appointment book, or electronic planner, not your wits.

   2. List your top three tasks for today . . . those with the highest risks and payoffs, as weighed against your goals.

   3. Schedule those top three tasks into the *best* (not the *earliest*) slots in your day.

4. Determine your *best* times: The times you know you can do the most important things well. When are your energy and accuracy highest? When can you get quiet or privacy for sensitive tasks? When can you get access to the help, equipment, data, or decision makers you need.

5. Slot your top three tasks before allotting time to any other demand.

6. Except for protecting your top 20 percent of tasks, leave most of your schedule "loose" for unexpected as well as second-tier jobs. But let nothing minor come between you and achievement of your top three tasks.

7. If you are selective enough, you can guarantee these three things get done; then you move down to second-level tasks of some value. Sometimes your top three tasks will use up most of your day; sometimes they will use only a few minutes each. But this "priority time" is sacred. Protect it!

Only "Majors" May Bump "Majors"

If you are forced to bump a major task—if a crisis or vital opportunity comes up—mark this "bump" on your schedule in a special color. For the rest of your career, use that color to mean only one thing: You bumped an item of major risk/value for something new that mattered more. If over a few weeks' time, you collect enough colored marks, you can ask yourself:

> Has my job changed? Are these crises or opportunities my new job? What are they worth? Are they temporary or have they replaced my former top tasks? Do I need help with this new volume?

Don't worry that you'll develop writer's cramp making colored marks. Remember—you only mark interruptions that are big enough to bump one of your top 20 percent priorities. But you've made the change visible, so you can decide whether you've got a temporary crisis or a new career.

Make Choices on Projects, Not Personalities

Let's look at our first two case studies to see how a manager and an administrative assistant get help with tough priority choices.

Case 1. Taming Two Titans

Proposed by Allen Sugarman, a construction manager for a large investment and finance institution.

I face continual priority conflicts between two senior V.P.s: Their huge projects cannot be handled in the same time period. If I mention staggering or delaying one phase for another, they explode and blame me for the conflicts. They rarely target each other. But they use me as a go-between. I feel like I'm always caught in the cross fire.

First Pass: Written Solutions From Seminar Colleagues

1. Remain neutral. Ask for a breather to research the schedule and other factors; then present your case in written or graphic form and ask for a decision. Puts more of the risk on them.

2. Get both bosses in a room to decide work flow priorities beforehand. Then note any changes or additions they make: Keep them responsible to authorize changes or delays in writing. The cause of delays must be laid at the right door.

3. Show relative risks in each request. Recommend options needed to accommodate each request, but show added costs and effects of new requests. If they stalemate, wash your hands and insist that they go to their next level for resolution.

Your Reaction: What Advice Would You Endorse or Add?

_____

_____

_____

_____

_____

Second Thoughts Expressed in Group Discussion

1. *Remain neutral: Research and present your case.* Put the risk on them. Good approach. Buy time to map out risks of running both jobs. Map some compromise or partial-completion solutions. Lay these out graphically for each boss, using project management graphics. For neutrality, make it standard procedure to identify all projects by code number, or project name. Detach the requester's name to reduce envious competition.

2. *Get both in a room.* Caution: Remember, it is not necessary to negotiate with both bosses at once, even if they are civil to one another. If they tend to gang up on you, why create

more tension for yourself? Get each to commit singly and in writing to realistic schedules you demonstrate.

3. *Demonstrate risks.* Excellent: Before starting projects, get senior VP's validation by assessing the relative risk and value of listed projects. (We'll illustrate this process shortly). Then offer options. As for *their escalating to the next level—* this is fine if you can convince senior VPs to go to their superiors. It is certainly too risky to attempt escalation yourself in any hierarchical organization where "going over heads" would be punished by various forms of solitary confinement.

Consensus Recommendations

Project conflicts naturally arise as events change. Reduce the number of times you must negotiate these conflicts by setting up risk/value standards that will take you through a lifetime of concurrent projects.

Figure 3 shows what such a chart might look like.

Figure 3. Risk-value standards for authorizing work.

SAMPLE RISK/VALUE CRITERIA (substitute yours)	*Request A*		*Request B*		*Request C*	
	Yes	No	Yes	No	Yes	No
A. Safety threat						
B. Cost over $ . . .						
C. Compliance penalty						
D. Income potential over $ . . .						
E. Top-tier customer						
F. Critical path item for major launch						
G. Team or tools only available now						

(Note: Deadline is not a criterion: It only breaks ties between two projects with same criteria.)

Expect Conflicts as Bosses Multiply

While Allen Sugarman had trouble serving two high-ranking managers, many secretaries and assistants must provide administrative help to four or more direct bosses and their staffs of sixty people or more, with no other secretarial help in sight. Here's a case in point:

Case 2. Five-Way Stretch

Proposed by Beryl Timmons, a top executive assistant in the hotel and hospitality field.

I assist five director-level bosses. Major priorities arrive all at once with impossible, competing deadlines. If I show any strain, I am seen as incompetent.

First Pass: Written Solutions From Seminar Colleagues

1. Ask the top manager to settle priority conflicts.

2. Get managers to choose the most vital item from their lists. Warn that some items must wait.

3. Let all five set priorities jointly, including downgrading things. If they won't downgrade anything, ask them to authorize your hiring help, either permanently or at foreseeable crunch times.

4. Get Human Resources (HR) or the office manager to hire temporary help for reliable coverage of peak loads. These five bosses will never back off, one for the other.

Your Reaction: What Advice Would You Endorse or Add?

_____

_____

_____

_____

_____

Second Thoughts Expressed in Group Discussion

1. *Get the top manager to settle conflicts.* This might work once, and then only if you enjoy excellent rapport with this senior boss. But these five-way conflicts will arise again and again. You risk irritating your senior boss into doing what you should have done in the first place: Set up a standard operating process to settle priority disputes. You set up a chart or menu of what is valid and what the lead times are. Then get an OK from all bosses, starting with the most senior.

2. *Get each manager to select top items from his list; bottom items wait.* Yes, it beats guessing, but you'll exhaust yourself doing this every time disputes arise. Instead, extend the exercise across each manager's whole workload: Get a ruling on a menu of each one's typical tasks for the year.

3. *Have all five downgrade things.* Yes, when managers see—on a wall chart—the relative risks that all competing items may incur, they may be willing to do regular priority planning. They may also see, with earlier warning, that part-time help is a necessity for peak-period coverage.

4. *Get HR or office manager to hire help: These five won't back off.* This responder has thrown in the towel on negotiating with managers. But her solution—getting HR to hire help without first getting joint priority agreement among senior managers—may expose HR to criticism and could waste the company's money at repeated chaotic intervals.

Consensus Recommendations

This assistant and her managers need to work out a cogent priority process that all can endorse. The chart should stay accessible—on the wall or on the computer. As work expands, the shakeout process can be repeated or even automated to stem arguments and keep tempers cool. All seminar members were concerned with Beryl's fear that her response to unreasonable demands could be read as incompetence. They warned her that accepting chronic overloads, staying late, and suffering in silence would risk performance errors. Be consistent in supporting the priority agreements reached jointly; then deliver on what you promise with firmness, just short of rigidity.

Exploit the Power of Graphic Solutions

Hallway conversations can be very helpful. For example, during a seminar break, a group of us helped a research analyst with a workload dilemma. Curt Nakimura handles research for a large property developer. Despite chronic overload problems brought on by assignments from three bosses—the CEO, marketing director, and the CFO—Curt faced worse threats. After a reorganization, and without consulting Curt, the CFO authorized the company controller to load Curt with even more detailed and deadline-driven work. Curt was baffled about how to refuse the work without looking incompetent or unwilling.

The hallway group asked so many questions about his direct lines of reporting that Curt went to a white board and started sketching to explain. In the process, he began to find solutions himself. We encouraged him to focus not on personalities but on the structure of the workloads. Curt saw that he should not ask *who* would do the restructured work but, instead, *how* the work could be reflowed more logically for himself or any helpers. Curt drew up three distinct possibilities that he took back to show the CEO and top team. In the process, Curt developed a much more detached view—a prerequisite for successful negotiating. Figure 4 shows his charts.

By illustrating his options, Curt was able to see this change as a chance to open negotiations on broader career concerns.

If you face a situation in which you must negotiate a more reasonable workload, you might want to adapt some of Curt's choices to your situation.

1. You could offer to specialize—assist fewer managers—devoting more of your time to a senior officer who has the power to protect you from the lower-value demands of junior managers. Senior managers have been known to do this for their own self-interest.

2. You could widen your coverage to help added managers—but only on selected high-impact matters. You might then delegate and supervise the handling of lower-impact matters by office helpers. Thus you would gain supervisory experience to add to your skills inventory. Yes, you'd have to negotiate this added expense, but you could prove that the cost of part-time help is far lower than the cost of the overtime you now incur. Even if you are an exceptional employee, your "unpaid" overtime incurs hidden costs in fatigue, stress, and risk of error.

3. You could suggest to your top-tier managers that they start delegating some matters to middle managers under their direction, moving peripheral issues to a lower operating level outside your domain.

Once you start sketching possibilities, you'll see more fresh options and you'll sound constructive, not defensive.

Use Triage to Avoid Traps

When I ask people how they justify their queuing decisions, they often admit:

My top boss comes first. Clout wins!
I want to be fair, so first come, first served.
I respond fast to emergencies.

Figure 4. Curt's work reflow options.

Plan A: Curt supports CEO and marketing director only.
Assumes new project administration for full load.
Detach CFO and Controller entirely; move work
to their new recruit within sixty days.

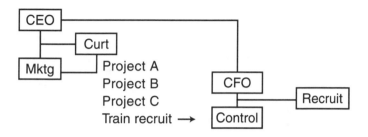

Plan B: Curt covers CEO, marketing director, CFO, and
controller but only on high-impact items. Curt gets
assistant for routine work.

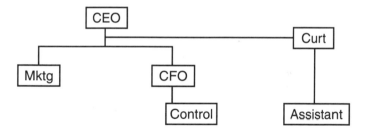

Plan C: Curt covers all top-tier managers: Finance delegates
selected projects to mid-level managers.

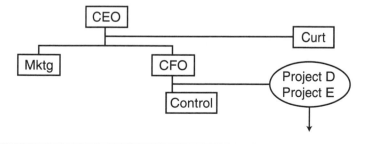

But there are the following traps in these choices:

- You may put your top boss first, but that boss has delegated vital work to others. Some pending assignments may outweigh the work the boss hands to you now. Ultimately, all work is being done on the orders of the top person. You need clearer signals.

- "First come, first served" works best when requests are roughly equal—as in a bakery or theater ticket line. But your requesters see themselves as unique.

- Finally, beware of validating work by "emergency." Some people will neglect common tasks until they become emergencies, just to get fast service. One Navy installation announced fast service for short-notice travel orders. To their chagrin, 60 percent of requesters waited until the twenty-four-hour deadline before initiating travel requests, so they could enjoy this faster service!

Instead, try a safer and smarter route: try *triage* on tasks—just as military field hospitals do in emergencies. Triage personnel first assess the gravity of an injury. Urgency breaks the tie between two brain injuries, but never between a brain injury and a broken toe. Triage personnel use urgency to decide which of two brain injuries will go first to the surgeon: The stronger patient may have to wait. But the patient with the broken toe will definitely wait, no matter how loudly he complains. The triage decision is made on risk (ability to survive), not on the urgency imagined by the patient.

Use the following to give yourself a better set of queuing rules:

- Perform tasks on validity, survivability, and magnitude of outcomes, not on the relative clout or anger of the requester.

- Abandon axioms like first come, first served.

- Question chronic emergencies, but validate real emergencies that arise from unforeseen threats beyond your control.

Some people and teams manage this way naturally, out of uncommonly good common sense. Many more are still trapped by powerful, angry squeaky wheels. To succeed at enforcing survivability, you must pursue it consciously and consistently in ways that can be understood by the major stakeholders in your widening circle of contacts.

Tool Kit: Chart Your Bosses' Bedrock Risks

Now, let's bring these principles home by working on your multi-boss situation. Consider charting valid priorities as you see them for one major boss (see Figure 5).

Figure 5. One boss's bedrock priorities.

Task or Responsibility	Risk/Value Order (High = 1)
☐ Budgets	6
☐ Forecasts	5
☐ Acquisitions	3
☐ Systems Upgrade	7
☐ Investments	1
☐ Currency Risk	2
☐ Audits	8
☐ Team Building	4

This CFO for an international company will shepherd two overseas mergers this year.

Her number 1 and number 2 risk/value items are largely controlled by outside companies or countries. She must monitor world events as they unfold and move quickly to maximize return on investment.

Next, items 3 and 4 are merger related: one operational, the other morale-based. Long- and short-term programs are in place.

Item 5 (with long-term effects) is riskier than item 6. Audits, number 8, is stable; meanwhile, item 7, though high-impact, is mostly delegated to able specialist managers.

Here's how you would go about it:

1. Imagine Figure 5 as the chart for one important boss whose work you handle. The eight most vital tasks for that boss's year are ranked in "survival" order as the boss would see it—that is, by long-term validity, not by urgency.

2. Get that person's agreement on the ranking order.

3. Next, do a chart for one or two additional bosses.

4. Then highlight areas where each person's top deadlines may collide. (Managers find this logistical map fascinating, especially if you show it *before* crises arise. They also find it nonthreatening.)

5. Now strategize (as a team, if applicable):

- Where must you clear competing tasks from the same active runway?
- Where could you anticipate data need or create templates for gradual completion so that few items would remain to plug in closer to the deadline (audit data, for example)?
- Where could you foresee or forestall overtime needs, by staffing earlier to prepare lengthy processes?

6. Discuss these charts regularly to prevent stressful surprises.

7. Keep these charts accessible, so you can update as workloads expand.

Your Reaction

For practice, fill in the blank chart (Figure 6). Plan to do added charts for additional bosses.

Armed with graphic clarity about priority needs, your bosses can comply with your newly agreed standards for getting work done. With clarity gained internally, you can move on to a more disparate group

Figure 6. Senior manager's vital risks for the year.

Task or Responsibility	Risk/Value Order (High = 1)
☐ _____	_____
☐ _____	_____
☐ _____	_____
☐ _____	_____
☐ _____	_____
☐ _____	_____
☐ _____	_____
☐ _____	_____

of requesters—your customers. If their demands pepper your work-days like incoming missiles, you may need our next set of tools.

Control Interruptions, but Enhance Interactions

Isn't it great how much you can get accomplished after regular work hours? *Sure,* you may be thinking, *that's because the phones are quiet, people have gone home, and I can do my job in peace.* But what is your job? Isn't it largely interacting with internal and external customers? If you are in sales, isn't customer service a major profit maker? If you're in engineering, isn't problem solving with clients a major role? If you are in personnel, HR, or research, isn't communication your major pathway for delivering results?

In jobs with multiple demands, you must balance two conflicting needs: the need to *interact* and the need to *concentrate.* Random interactions destroy concentration. So it is the randomness you must reduce. Begin modestly. Seek only to reduce the worst 20 percent of your interruptions so you can concentrate on research, analysis, calculation, writing, drafting, designing, editing, and above all, decision making on behalf of those interrupters. What can you do to carve out some concentration time?

At first, interruptions appear uncontrollable, unavoidable, and unpredictable. Managers ask, "How can I tell who will call or walk in?" True, if you look at interrupters singly, you can't tell who they will be or what they'll be looking for. But when you study them in aggregate, you see patterns . . . patterns showing heavier interruptions at certain times of the day or the month, patterns based on cyclical or seasonal events, and interruptions you invited by publishing announcements or advertisements. By backing up just far enough to see interrupters in aggregate, you'll see patterns that you can bring under control or serve in batches.

- Analyze those interruption patterns.
- Create clear policies on when and why people should interact. (For example: *"Voice mail inquiries left by 10:00 A.M. will be answered by 3:00 P.M."* or *"For help on applying the new software, call the hot line or attend the clinics to be held daily at 11:00 A.M. Do not call fellow employees with random questions."*)
- Provide self-help options rather than direct contact with you.
- Provide dedicated appointment times and offer the best service then.

If you can see a pattern, you can provide services to alter them. Lacking a policy or failing to provide channels will force you to take all comers randomly. If you must squander energy on small, random matters, you get too tired to handle big ones. Spot the patterns and create alternate channels: so you can give energy to your projects and caring service to your clients.

Tool Kit: Use the Dot Chart to Pinpoint Patterns

Time management gurus suggest using time logs. I declare logs a nuisance. They are not selective enough. First, you are asked to record everything that happens; then you have to spend time interpreting your random notes at day's end. This leaves you less time for actual work. I recommend, instead, that you focus on spotting only the worst 20 percent of interruptions. Log these and allow yourself to tolerate the rest. You'll get relief right away when you tolerate 80 percent of interruptions instead of 100 percent.

There's a sample of a selective interruption log in Figure 7. We call it a *dot chart* because you use dots to record selected interruptions under preset headings. If an event continues for more than fifteen minutes or so, you extend the dot, dropping a line down to the next time period. Dots signal brief events; lines signal longer ones. Trust yourself to know which categories or types of interruption are worth recording. The following list gives some examples:

- Same question from too many people
- Callers who want to hold while you do exhaustive research
- Late warning by others will default a delivery
- Work tossed at you too close to deadline
- E-mail glut (over one hundred messages per day)
- Misdirected inquiries

Whatever your irritants, be selective in charting. Never track more than five columns, and don't be fastidious about it. You're looking for obvious patterns, not perfect numbers. Even if you forget to record events half the time, you'll still detect patterns worth fixing.

Once you spot a pattern, you can devise helpful options.

- For seasonal interruptions when people's questions are legitimate but the flow is too heavy:
    —De-randomize: offer a "clinic"; set a time or place.
    —Preempt: Offer a "clinic page" on your electronic bulletin board where frequently asked questions can be answered for everyone.
- To reserve some quiet time:

Figure 7. Selective interruption log.

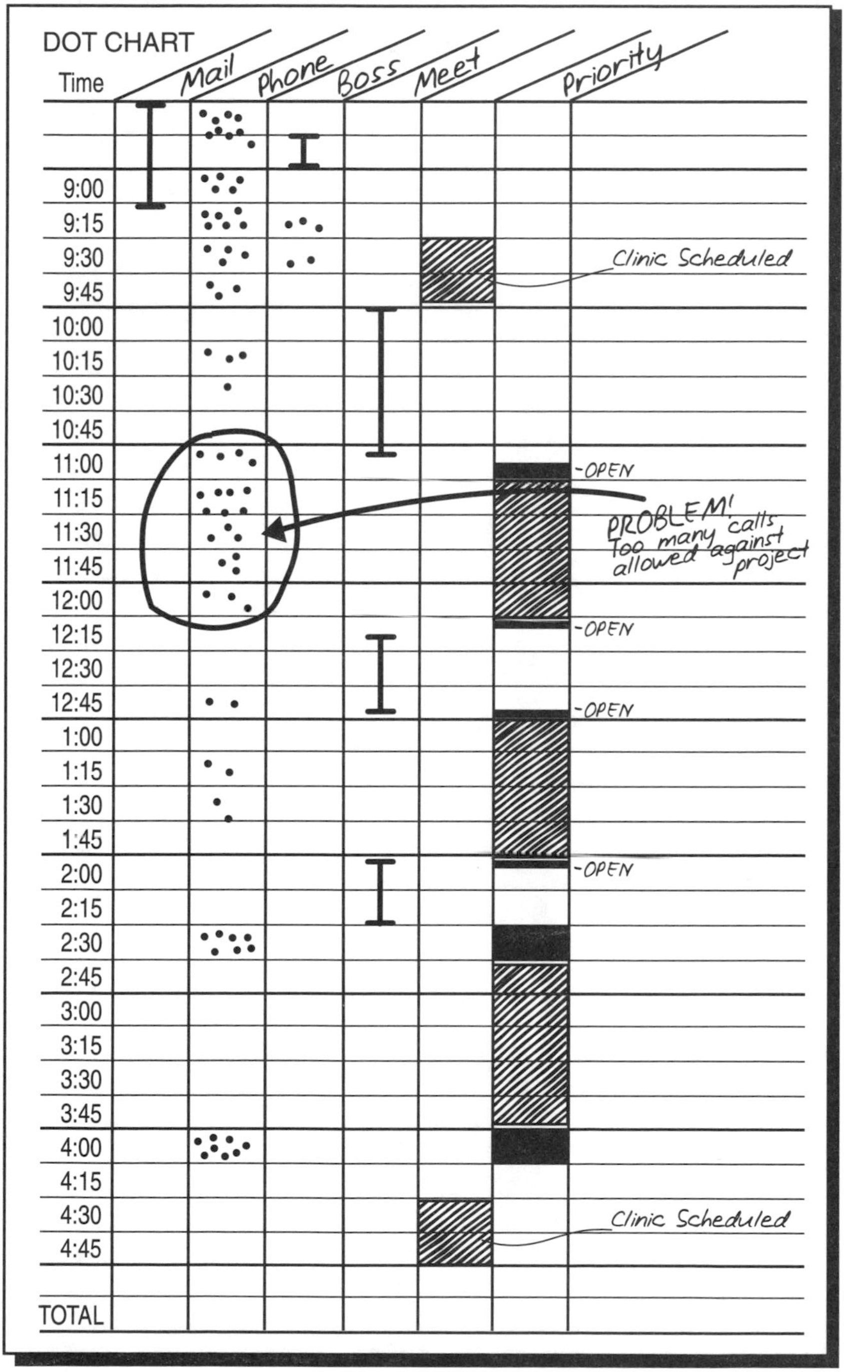

(continues)

Figure 7. *(continued)*

DOT CHART Time							
9:00							
9:15							
9:30							
9:45							
10:00							
10:15							
10:30							
10:45							
11:00							
11:15							
11:30							
11:45							
12:00							
12:15							
12:30							
12:45							
1:00							
1:15							
1:30							
1:45							
2:00							
2:15							
2:30							
2:45							
3:00							
3:15							
3:30							
3:45							
4:00							
4:15							
4:30							
4:45							
TOTAL							

—Block out two or three periods per day in red for "must do" work. These periods can be interrupted only for matters of greater weight.

—Provide service: Be sure to bracket any red zones with a brief green zone when people can reach you freely.

■ Give people some contact time in order to get yourself some quiet time.

■ Use desk signs or cubicle signs with a positive message, such as "Deadline work in progress: Call extension 20 . . . or use e-mail. Response guaranteed by 3:00 P.M."

If you want more quiet time, leave clear greeting messages on your voice mail so people will know when to expect replies. If people know you will reply at 3:00, they may stay off your voice mail until then.

An Illuminating Interview: **Negotiating for Life**

Some solid ideas about multitasking come from Alison R, a twelve-year veteran in the space exploration business. As a safety engineer, she reports to two in-line supervisors and three Safety Panel chairpeople from different organizations. She balances all this deftly, enjoying her multiple-demand situation. As she puts it:

The biggest advantage of my having multiple bosses is personal growth. I've learned so much about myself and my abilities by serving and negotiating with different kinds of people simultaneously. I've grown significantly in confidence and self-esteem as well as in the ability to think on my feet and be diplomatic, which used to be hard for me.

Her greater challenge, as she describes it:

Running my family life with three small kids, two with disabilities, is like a second business, no less important during 8:00 to 5:00 than my paid job—and a lot more demanding after hours. This means dealing with teachers, therapists, social workers, and doctors to obtain services for the two children with disabilities. Daily therapy, health care advocacy, and research work must be done: I must match my response to the professional's style in ways that ensure compliance from that person. I use leadership skills in the absence of real power to get the best help or information efficiently.

At the same time, I must excel enough at my paid job to keep my supervisors as happy with my work as they are with my peers. This often involves juggling—putting items aside briefly, managing major issues—and then switching back again quickly when necessary.

Asked about ethical differences at work, Alison had no complaints.

Very rarely have I had an issue at work that causes me to question my supervisor's ethics. Coping with varied person-alities means responding flexibly. Often, I must change my approach from detail-oriented to big-picture within mo-ments. In a meeting at work, I'm expected to be accurate, detailed, and concise. Conversely, in my child advocacy work, diplomacy is paramount.

As for tools, Alison uses some flexible workplace privileges, in-cluding a home computer and fax modem as well as a pager. E-mail is her most frequently used communication tool.

I send e-mail to distribution lists to keep all bosses informed simultaneously on what I am working on. I always keep my alternates informed so they can be effective in getting things done. Keeping informed at work is no problem: Office chat does the trick. However, keeping informed on the latest dis-ability laws and issues that might benefit my kids is a chal-lenge. Kids whose parent don't do research to keep current don't get the best services. If I could afford more help at home, I could do research, letter writing, and deal with insur-ance company mistakes at 10:00 P.M. instead of 2:00 A.M., leaving me fresher during the day at work.

Alison also uses a Franklin Planner and her MS Schedule software, which she shares electronically with her husband, a full-time partner at work and at home.

Whatever I learn and do on behalf of our kids my husband must also know, so he can perform on it when necessary.

Alison's "secret weapon" for success in multitasking:

I go with the flow, relax, and don't sweat the small stuff. I do my best and don't beat myself up for what doesn't get done. And especially, I don't tie my self-esteem to my job and what happens there. That doesn't mean I care less about the work or job satisfaction; I simply am no longer destroyed by things like stray comments or requests to do something over. Un-derstanding the management styles of my bosses and flexing my own approaches can help me to meet their needs better. I no longer take what they say personally, nor do I get defensive. In the same way, I treat my advocacy work like a business. I detach from the emotional side in order to do it efficiently with as little negative stress as possible.

Triumphs and Turnarounds: Pacific Interval

Here's a favorite story on the virtues of pointing out risks early and graphically for customers who get overwhelmed. Ella Spacco manages the shipping of personal effects and household goods for military personnel being transferred from the mainland to Hawaii. She gets many panicky calls from people who arrive in Honolulu by plane and wonder why their furniture, scheduled to arrive by boat, has not preceded them. Are these people stupid? No . . . just harried by the pressure of moving home and family across the Pacific, sometimes with little notice and less money. Nonetheless, Ella gets irritated when people don't bother to read the shipping contracts that spell out cargo arrival dates. (After all, they had agreed to these dates when they signed the documents.) At the seminar, she waved a sample of the document for us to see: It was tissue-thin, legal-size paper covered with tiny 6-point type. I took it in hand and squinted at it.

Ding! Her bell went off. She went back to work and designed a simple postcard with hand-drawn artwork of great charm. She drew a little airplane flying from the West Coast to Honolulu: The plane towed a banner saying "six hours." Below that, she drew a big boat sailing over the waves for Honolulu: It towed a banner with the words "ten days." A bold headline instructed: "Keep these dates in mind when you schedule your move." That card was the last thing she handed to customers, and the final thing she reminded them to check when planning their move. From then on, she experienced a dramatic drop in complaint calls. Ella sent me a sample of her quaint, simple artwork, and I carried it around with me until later audiences wore it out. I still enjoy this tattered souvenir of her time-saving triumph.

What About You?

Is there a simple customer service message you should get across in order to reduce some of the random demand on your e-mail, voice mail, or walk-in traffic? Start sketching your own postcard!

Summary: Ten Tools and Techniques to Try

1. *Adopt a multi-tasking mind-set.* Get satisfaction from making progress on many goals rather than getting completion on only

one. Work to derive satisfaction from entrepreneurship. Run your job like a business you own. Then welcome and pursue multiple customers to ensure long-term job security.

2. *Next, use Pareto's Law to rank projects by survivability.* That is, guarantee the item with the highest risk and the highest value and then rank them downward by risk descent. The items with high value but lower, stabilized risk can often be delegated or automated.

3. *Get consulting time, regular and reliable, with each boss and customer.* This can be brief, face-to-face, phoned, or electronic, but it must be reserved and uninterrupted.

4. *Map out options for giving support.* Which matters will you handle for each boss? At which points must you stay in the loop for good coordination?

5. *Use graphic task-maps.* That way, newly added projects can be weighed against those already slated. To restructure large workloads, focus on task flows, not personalities. Map work flows logically before staffing up for coverage.

6. *Negotiate early.* The moment your good sense tells you a demand is unrealistic, offer to estimate the load. Then give your assessment and suggest a safer option. Don't worry that you'll be seen as negative when you express doubts about a demand. You can say to a disgruntled requester: "I make it my policy never to expose anyone to a blind risk. Let me point out some risks hidden in your request."

7. *Tool kit.* At intervals, chart each boss's priorities. Renegotiate whenever you see two major priorities conflicting in the same time period. With multiple bosses, take the time to chart conflicting priorities across a wide menu of expected tasks. Set up protocols so you won't have to fight out each conflict singly. Negotiate to extend deadlines, get help, shrink the scope, or reduce the level of detail required on conflicting projects. Do all these things to avoid last-minute defaults.

8. *Tool kit.* Use the dot chart (Figure 7) to track and stop your worst 20 percent of interruptions. Then use signs and simple instructions to help interrupters to do the work for themselves.

9. *Use electronic and graphic displays.* These can be used to keep yourself and others informed on priority conflicts and resolutions.

10. *Liberate yourself from the need to please everyone.* Your self-esteem must not come solely from your job.

In these ways, you see and demonstrate consequences with clarity and concern. You also base your service quality on consistent principles, rather than on hot-button reactions.

2 Conquer the Communication Crunch

Have multiple workloads and deadlines forced you to isolate your-self in your cube? How much of your team interplay has gone virtual? Some people would live a lifetime on electronic messaging alone, but isolation threatens team unity and coordination.

You Still Need Meetings

To keep teamwork alive, you need to assemble. Don't sacrifice meet-ings—improve them; keep them short! Assure a regular, reliable time and place to gather once a week. You can meet fast—on your feet, when necessary. But there are some things done better "live" than by electronic chat or management fiat, such as work planning and coordinating, creative problem solving, victory celebrations, and new policy development. Items affecting fairness—gain sharing, task allo-cation, task coverage, tough duty rotations—need team debate.

Create Shared Graphics

Whether you meet face-to-face, by teleconference, or by electronic bulletin board, you need to create some vital graphics that can be posted on any available wall to communicate instantly.

- *Checklists for mutual support.* Just as airline crews use check-lists to assure flight safety, good work teams use graphic check-lists to assure reliable levels of performance. Progress charts, milestone charts, and Gannt charts will help team members to stay focused on important targets. If you keep all your tools electronic, you'll find that some people ignore them. They sim-ply never click on them. If you post them on the wall, more people see and remember them.
- *Standard signaling devices.* Use images unique to the team.

Code words, colors, or numbers can convey instant meanings. Some teams use metal flags on their cubes to denote "in" or "quiet time." Others fly a balloon to signal milestones reached or sales made. Silent signals—instant celebrations!

■ *Designate a specific location.* A pennant or signaling spot can convey heads-up messages. Bulletin boards, kiosks, *Post-it*® notes, maps, clipboards, and wall signs help everyone keep up-to-date, no matter how much data may clutter one's computer screen. One Bank of America unit posts the production target for the night above the entry door. The night-shift workers come in knowing what they have to do. Crazy prizes are offered for tough targets, and these are eagerly pursued. Graphic devices add fun and verve to the workplace while bolstering team unity.

You Can Still Get Private Time

"Got a minute?" How many times today will an interrupter stop by or phone you with that inane question? Even if they can see you staring at your computer screen, fielding phone calls, or dashing out the door, they still ask if you're busy. What they really mean is *"Am I more important than whatever you're doing now?"*

If you care about your job, you want to answer yes to every requester; you want to chase opportunities and solve problems as they arise. Yet you must still execute plans and meet deadlines. The dot chart shown in Chapter One helps you see *whether* you need to negotiate; this chapter shows you *how.* First, let's lay down two basic principles.

You Need Never Ignore a Caller

While companies everywhere have allowed workers to overuse voice mail, essentially ignoring all callers for hours, you can make better choices. Your contacts are vital: They need respect, help, data, and reassurance. But do they need *you* and do they need you *now*?

How can you rechannel customer inquiries so people can unburden themselves, assured that on-time service will be provided? How can you continue your work uninterrupted to meet your preset, promised targets? How can you provide the greatest good to the greatest number of clients? Making those day-by-day decisions is the basis for communication. It's not the words you say, it's the fundamental decision behind those words . . . the "survivability" decision that you must make up front.

Each time you are interrupted, glance at your top three tasks that you have written down (see Chapter One). (Some people jot these onto a sticky note and affix it to the computer as each day begins.) You have a visual cue on what really counts, no matter how involved you get with interruptions. This cue prompts you to ask how this interruption stacks up against your must-do goals for today. If the interruption cannot match or outclass your preset requirements, you still have the following options:

■ *Acknowledge and postpone.* You might say to the interrupter: *"Thanks for telling me about this problem. This would take twenty to thirty minutes to resolve. Let's regroup this afternoon at 4:00. I'm on another deadline now. . . . No? How about tomorrow morning at 10:00? Meanwhile, I'll get the research started."* (You jot a note to yourself and go back to your top job.)

■ *Acknowledge and delegate.* You might respond in friendly fashion: *"Yes. I see. I've assigned this subject to Sue Kearney. This is her specialty. I'm no longer up-to-date on it. Here's her pager number."* You've now delegated this contact, even if Sue's voice mail is the receptor for now. Do not voice opinions nor get further involved.

■ *Acknowledge and empower.* You might reply: *"Yes. I see how vital this is to you. And there's some preparation you need to do so that I—or whoever helps you—can get started fast. Here's what to do now . . ."*

If you cannot help the caller now, but there's something he can be doing to make the process go faster—then get him busy on his own behalf. You instruct the caller how to start until you or a referral can handle the problem. You've removed some of the caller's powerlessness—helped him make progress at a time when you could not help directly.

■ *Acknowledge and refer.* Sometimes, you know how to help, or the caller is a friend, so you're tempted to wade in, even though it's none of your business. You could say: *"Sounds important, but that's a matter for the employee assistance team* (or the tax team, etc.)." You can help link a caller with the authorized team. In this way, you show him how to go direct next time. Take a moment to write a little note or an e-mail to remind your friend of the direct route. Write yourself out of the loop.

You Need Not Deal With Distress on the Spot

You can use these same techniques when your subordinates come crying to you over some incident. If you let them talk while they're angry or outraged, they may say something in the heat of the moment that they will later regret. Here's a scenario: Suppose Doris comes in, bad-mouthing a fellow employee. You could hear her out and counsel her now, or you could say:

This sounds important, Doris . . . too important to deal with now when we might be interrupted. Let's sit down at 2:00 when it's quieter. Until then, would you be willing to take an index card and write down the *outcomes* you want to see from our discussion? If you focus less on what happened, and more on what you want to see happen next, we'll start closer to the target you need when we do sit down.

This approach helps Doris to do some homework. It helps her to stop focusing on accusations and start focusing on needs. It also buys her time to cool off. Your intent is to help her make a request to you that you can say yes to. In your interview, later, ask her to omit the other person, altogether, and to speak only of herself—what she needs and wants.

In fact, one VP at Bank of America liked this notion so much that he had those words printed on a sign that faces his guest chair:

Make Me a Request I Can Say Yes To.

His team members arrive better prepared and more positive, even after disturbing incidents.

Consider Time and Priority Management as Two Distinct Things

What comes to your mind when someone mentions the word *priorities*? Do you picture conflicting workloads, deadlines, and schedules? If so, you are thinking about time management, not priority management. Time management involves scheduling: deciding *when* to do work; priority management involves validating: deciding *whether* to do work.

You can practice time management solo, increasing self-discipline. But priority management is a team sport; it always requires negotiation. That means you must communicate in ways that take foresight and courage, especially if the other parties outrank or outgun you.

Begin: Do Your Homework on New Standards

To manage priorities effectively, you'll need to consider, adopt, and negotiate some startling new standards. Like many mid-level managers and assistants you may argue:

Who am I to set or change standards? I've been given orders! My bosses and customers expect me to comply—to just do it, without debate.

Sure they do! And you will comply in every case where the risks are manageable. But when you serve multiple bosses, you are their first and only line of defense against major defaults. You—not your multiple bosses—will be the first to spot major conflicts and risks in aggregate and in a way that no single requester can. So—expected or not—if *you* don't negotiate, who will? If you don't negotiate, your clients must accept the consequences of defaults without due warning. You may be blamed, but the client always takes the consequences. Unless managers allow you to warn and offer options (i.e., negotiate), your clients will be taking their consequences blindly.

Some Worn Standards to Scuttle

To adopt new priority management rules for yourself, you will have to override some of the most deeply embedded ideas in business:

Do first things first.
The early bird catches the worm.
The squeaky wheel gets the grease.

If your requesters expect you to surrender to these outworn ideas, you'll need to reeducate them on these issues, one at a time.

Do First Things First

Ben Franklin is said to have advised this in *Poor Richard's Almanac.* Not so. He advised his readers, "**Plan** *first things first.*" He defined *first things* as essential things, not urgent things. He proposed that we provide the best time slot or facility for the most essential tasks in the day. That's how you arrange your day. Even when you open up for interrupters, you still protect the essential slots unless the new item outweighs them.

The Early Bird Catches the Worm

Not unless this bird brings the most legitimate risks and the highest potential value! Being early is not enough in itself. If you are first at the antique show but cannot afford the item, the dealer may wait until the show is nearly over before offering a reduced price. Being early does not help. You may be first to request a luxury hotel room for the company conference, but if the CEO books space later than you—and the best rooms are gone—your premier room may be "borrowed" for the CEO, and you may find yourself at some other hotel. Be gently honest with those who still embrace this axiom. *Early* does not weigh in against *high risk* and *high value.* How many points out of one hundred will you give to being early? Be ready to say it.

The Squeaky Wheel Gets the Grease

By whining, some requesters may force a worker to meet their demands now, but workers will seldom tolerate this a second time. You have probably witnessed some frustrated worker, avoiding an argument but moving the squeaky wheel's memo to the bottom of the pile. The worker then apologizes and suggests that the complainer take the complaint to a higher level. If the squeaky wheel has become famous for it, those at higher levels also fail to sympathize. In this way, the world gets its revenge on squeaky wheels. Direct action is better: Perhaps you can recruit a more powerful figure to teach requesters that their demands are out of line and that continuance of these behaviors may get them shut off or criticized in their next performance review. Some bosses teach this lesson to outside customers, too, preferring to lose a customer who won't obey reasonable rules.

As a professional, you have better choices than bowing to outworn axioms. Work with your team to set clear standards on the performance levels that requesters can expect. Publicize these standards: It demonstrates their fairness. Take a proactive rather than punitive, reactive stance. Invite participation by your customers and clients: People tend to obey rules that they helped create.

Six New Standards to Adopt and Announce

Standard 1

- To earn the number one priority slot, a task must have both the highest risk and the highest value—that is, highest validity.

Standard 2

- Urgency is secondary to validity. Urgency can break the tie only between tasks of the same risk and value level—tasks of equal consequence.

Standard 3

- Clout is a secondary factor, too, even at the CEO level. Often, a competing task submitted from a lower level has greater consequence to the company at large than something submitted now by the CEO. If you remain silent, you expose the CEO to a blind risk. At least give the senior officer a chance to see what his request may be "bumping." Then the CEO will exercise decision-making power in short order.

Standard 4

- Don't pit short-range tasks (rocks) against large long-range projects (boulders). Instead, equalize the tasks and intervals: Divide the large long-range project into shorter-interval tasks. Most people make the mistake of tackling many trivial, short-term tasks, hoping to clear a big chunk of time to execute the large project. But the big chunk of time never comes. Stop! Break the big task down into smaller tasks. Now, pit rocks against rocks. Consequences will help you see your choices. You'll vote for the tasks that connect with the big outcomes—not the ones with the quick but low-merit results. You'll start seeing trivia for what they are—tasks to be farmed out or delegated to lower-cost performers.

Standard 5

- Give the same scrutiny to *prevention* versus *reaction.* Regardless of task size or apparent urgency, focus on ultimate consequences; otherwise, you'll spend your professional life fighting small brush fires and never coming off the fire line. For example, if you put out a lot of small hillside brush fires but wait for a big chunk of time to plant acres of fire-retardant ground cover, you'll get acres of mud slides with the next rain. You'll lurch from one type of emergency to another, exhausting yourself and never creating safety. Instead, divide your replanting effort into smaller areas—with shorter time segments. Make gains across both fronts—fire fighting and ground cover planting. You will accomplish the fire-prevention effort, one small hillside at a time, and next summer you'll be called to fewer brush fires. Consequences are everything.

Standard 6

- Let actions have their consequences. The requester who causes chronic emergencies must pay a premium for emergency services rendered. The principle is blunt: If offenders pay nothing, they reform nothing. If you offer yourself as a rescuer, always doing "silent saves" for callous requesters, you are the only one taking the strain. So begin: Allow consequences to fall where they should. You need not force consequences; nature will take its course. Just don't take actions that muffle consequences for others. Warn, then stand firm.

As an example . . . suppose you need data from a lateral group to complete a project. Their data arrive late and incomplete. If you make it your practice to correct their data, you increase your department's costs while reducing theirs. Was that management's intent? By overperforming for some people, you may unwittingly cheat others and your company. If your efforts to restore fairness are overruled from on high, you may have to comply. But seek management support to end expensive and irrational rescues.

Case 3. Unrealistic Deadlines

Presented by Eric Hanson, production manager for an industrial manufacturer.

Sales and customer service units set unrealistic deadlines for us. They have direct contact with the client. When we point out the risks in their unrealistic deadlines or specifications, they argue hotly that the customer is always right, and that we are there to make it happen.

First Pass: Written Solutions From Seminar Colleagues

1. Escalate. You've invested enough time arguing.

2. Representatives from all departments meet with the customer. Educate them all on realistic production choices. Ask them to select key requirements. Meet those! Compromise on lesser items.

3. Warn sales and customer service; then carry out your warning. If your best efforts really cannot meet those deadlines, you will simply deliver late, leaving it to sales and customer service to make it right with the customer, or lose the customer.

4. Chart some clear, agreed standard production times and lead-time minimums. Provide these charts to the sales and customer service folks so they can come closer to reality with all customers "up front." Stop wearing yourself out arguing every deal on a case-by-case basis. Then say what you mean, and mean what you say.

Your Reaction: What Advice Would You Endorse or Add?

_____

_____

_____

Second Thoughts Expressed in Group Discussion

1. *Escalate?* No, not until you have exhausted other potential solutions like those described below.

2. *All departments meet with customer.* Depends on your company's policy about keeping production discussions in-house and leaving customer relations primarily to sales and customer service. There are different risks to each approach. But certainly, your production group needs to set clear, unequivocal standards jointly with lateral sales and customer service groups.

3. *Warn sales and customer service of pending default.* The last-ditch solution: Recommended only after you've done all you can with suggestion 2. Whenever you are forced to deliver late, acknowledge this with open regret and frustration. Don't let defaults become routine. This would bring decay and eventual losses to your company.

4. *Provide standard lead-time tools.* This is the most rational approach. Develop a set of production standards and lead times, agreed to internally by production, sales, and customer service, that could be adjusted only by senior management fiat.

Consensus Recommendations

Course members are appalled that so many companies still do an ad hoc debate for each customer or job rather than hammer out a realistic set of standards for quality, quantity, and costs on typical kinds of work. It is a further irony of management life that in some organizations senior managers seem to prefer default to debate. Lower-level managers must assume the courage to test this assumption, especially earlier in the process.

You Need Priority Protocols

With agreed protocols on work standards, you should walk a smoother and shorter path to realism for customers, bosses, and lateral groups. But once outside the realm of production—in harder-to-measure areas like administration and personnel—arguments about realistic workloads can escalate personal tensions between levels, as you'll see in the case that follows.

Case 4. The Workaholic Boss

Presented by Fran Spengler, a top-level administrative assistant.

How do I handle a workaholic boss who gets involved in everything and adds to my workload significantly even though I assist other VPs? This is a manager I admire and whose ambition will take her far, but she's taking more than her fair share of my time.

First Pass: Written Solutions From Seminar Colleagues

1. Expect workaholism in a dedicated boss. Her ambition may take you far, also. Get with it!

2. Do all you can for her and leave it at that if you have other people to assist.

3. Get on-call help, or ask her to do more of her own work in a pinch. She might be willing to do more rough drafting or better expense preparation when you are both chasing the same deadline. My boss—also a VP—pitches in when I ask. This may be time to review the bidding with all your VPs together.

4. Here, people get to *keep* their jobs by doing all that is listed on the job description: They get promoted by doing *more.* If you need light duty, you need a lower-level slot where you will get light appreciation and light pay.

Your Reaction: What Advice Would You Endorse or Add?

Second Thoughts Expressed in Group Discussion

1. *Workaholic?* Avoid labeling people workaholics, unless they call themselves by that name and invite you to do

so. Even then, hesitate! Labeling is an unattractive practice. Your boss may be, just as you see her, ambitious, dedicated, and truly busy. An ambitious boss can run you ragged, no doubt. But she may help you rise. Make a convincing case for any lower-cost help you may need, and hang on!

2. *Do all you can.* Yes, but discuss it. Workers who occupy a chair from nine until five, doing "all they can" and then going home at day's end, are deciding for themselves what work levels are possible. Others may be performing much better. Don't hide. Come to an agreement with your boss. In your chat, you can express goodwill toward this boss, which always helps in a high-pressure relationship. You can inform her about your total workload: She may be unaware how much you must do for other VPs. Don't seek to dump her if you admire her. Instead, ask her to go to bat for lower-level help that would report to you.

3. *Get help but seek boss collaboration.* Sensible advice. The assistant and boss who engage in partnering tend to negotiate ongoing workloads continually.

4. *Doing more is required for promotion.* A tough-minded answer, coming from secretarial battle experience at VP and higher levels. It's no picnic up there. Fran understands this, having succeeded with her other VPs. She objects only to the disproportionate use of her time by a single, busy VP. Paint the boss a picture; take it from there.

Consensus Recommendations

Back to answer number 3: reapportion time, anticipate rising needs, make your commitments clear, seek help below you so you can serve those above you. You might also need to create a tool that helps managers clarify their expectations.

Tool Kit: The Work-Worry-Warn Chart for Commitment

If you provide services for a number of senior managers, chances are that they don't feel equally served at all times; they may complain, obliquely or directly, that they don't get an equitable share of your time. You might benefit everyone by installing a tool that preserves clear priorities and keeps workloads realistic for multi-boss workers.

Start posting a *work-worry-warn chart.* It's a simple graphic device to help busy performers track progress along several fronts at the same time. The heart of this chart is the notion that it's foolhardy to give or accept a deadline unless you first agree on an estimate.

Let's take Georgie as an example: Let's say she does drafting or legal research (or whatever) for three high-ranking managers. From now on, Georgie prepares the sheet shown in Figure 8.

When Georgie accepts Assignment A, she asks for a due date, and an estimate of the necessary time to complete the task. If the manager doesn't have an estimate, they use common sense or experience to assign a tentative estimate. Then, as she works, Georgie tracks her progress. How many hours has she invested in the work? By one-quarter or midway through the task, she checks her time use. If she has used up four hours by midpoint, but the total estimate was six hours, she can see she's going to be late, and she can warn Manager A while there is still time to adjust the schedule. Georgie can gauge her progress against deadlines on Assignments B, C, and D, too. She can seek whatever adjustment she needs, leaving managers negotiating room. People who use project management software would consider this tool an obvious must. But, too often, people in administrative work use only vague rules of thumb or memory to guide work; they fail to keep estimates, and they default at an alarming rate.

Using a simple device like Georgie's, you impress your multiple bosses on three fronts:

1. That you accept multitasking as your responsibility.
2. That you need an estimate, as well as a deadline, for any major task; otherwise, you cannot gauge your progress against the clock or calendar.
3. That merely working well from nine to five is your minimum intent. That planning and organizing—for you—will include the

Figure 8. Work-worry-warn chart.

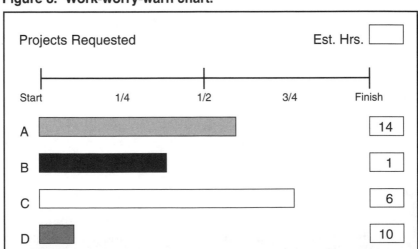

responsibility to *work, worry, and warn* requesters of impending shortfalls while there is still time to adjust or seek help.

What about you? Could you use this quick tool to clarify expectations with your multiple bosses? Would they be grateful that you are willing to work, worry, and warn them to prevent defaults on important team goals?

Meetings: The Most Frequently Mentioned Time Wasters

In surveys of industrial, business, and government managers, complaints abound about the stress of attending too many meetings with too few satisfactory results. The following case is an example.

Case 5. Meetings Mangle Time

Presented by Carol Chen, a senior software designer.

Unannounced meetings keep bumping other vital tasks and wrecking my work schedule. I spend hours per week calling or e-mailing team members and clients to reschedule deliverables as meetings chew up our time. Many of our meetings are called before solid data are ready for debate. We'd like the project managers to take more risks on their own and get farther down the road before involving everyone. But the president insists that meetings keep us unified as a team. He thrives on turbulence, but it's the designers who must manage or perform the detailed work. We hate this "planning by committee."

First Pass: Written Solutions From Seminar Colleagues

1. Start keeping a record so that a pattern emerges; pinpoint which meetings are the big offenders, those called without sufficient data for decision makers. Then use this record to turn down these meetings. For meetings with topics you do care about, you can ask for agendas beforehand, offer suggestions in writing, and study the minutes afterward, so you can still be involved without being there.

2. Appoint stand-ins for certain subject areas, a list of people selected formally to sit in for you and to vote in your place.

3. Request that all meetings carry strictly timed agendas. Then attend for only those moments when your participation

or vote is required. Some companies adopt this floating atten-
dance because it optimizes time use for each senior manager,
whose time is costly.

4. Our company has standardized meeting times and
agendas. Meetings are always held at the same time (late
day) to encourage people to keep them short. Our managers
know that, barring a true emergency, they can depend on having almost all day free to work, with meetings preplanned for
day's end.

5. My CEO sends a sort of "sealed bid" to meetings she
cannot attend. That way her opinion is known (and it carries a
lot of weight), but she does not feel obliged to be there to hear
all the preliminaries firsthand. People who want her approval
tend to line up her support beforehand; then the meeting is
held to convince the rest of the troops. This also saves her
from embarrassing questions, such as "What do you think?"
in front of a large group meeting. She's had a chance to think
things over in private or to consult whoever she likes. Her written decisions tend to be supported because they make sense.

Your Reaction: What Advice Would You Endorse or Add?

_____

_____

_____

_____

_____

Second Thoughts Expressed in Group Discussion

1. *Keep records on wasted meetings.* The dot chart
would be a simple tool for this. Members could keep a "dot
track" for meetings headed as follows:

    a. Needed to be there   b. Waste of time
               c. Send stand-in

Keep it simple enough and the emerging patterns help meetings improve. In some companies, all attendees at meetings
are asked to fill out a quick critique at the close of the meeting:
They answer questions about the level of detail available, the
expertise of the presenters, the quality of the data, and its
readiness for a vote by decision makers. Keep score on the
patterns of readiness of certain meetings: You can quickly validate the good ones, and kill or correct the bad ones.

2. and 3. *Send stand-ins. Require timed agendas.* These make sense. Many companies follow both rules to get more decisions made at the lowest possible level.

4. *Standardized meeting times.* Whether your company uses end-of-day or some other standard time, this practice allows better planning and fewer ad hoc interruptions. The downside of late-day meetings: Some decision makers are too weary to vote. Poor decisions made by tired people tend to get overturned in subsequent meetings. It might make better sense to cite certain times as "off limits" for meetings. Protect some "quiet time" in which all members of a team or a whole organization can really push important work through.

5. *Premeeting data and sealed bids.* Another good choice for senior managers. On some topics, the boss prefers one-on-one chats or e-mails with proposers, who can then take that endorsement into meetings. If the CEO's written vote would cut off debate prematurely, you might need to think this choice through again. Experiment. Different meeting practices carry different risks.

Consensus Recommendations

More than half the managers we poll rank too many meetings as damaging their top-priority projects, so getting meetings in control is a worthy task for every team. Above all, your team should take the time to list matters *not* suitable for meetings. An example would be meetings held to spread the blame and meetings held to get opinions from people before data are gathered. Your team could also set some simple house rules about the meetings; some typical ones we see in practice are the following:

- All meetings must have timed agendas and cannot run overtime.
- Members will not interrupt; they will reserve questions for question time.
- Speakers will adhere to the schedule, preparing their remarks and handouts to fit the available time.

Make your own house rules to fit your culture: Enforce them to reduce stress and waste. Here's a useful comment from a newly promoted government manager, citing the benefits of controlling meeting mayhem.

I am writing more e-mails and calling fewer meetings. In the past, I left every meeting with a *greater* load,

which my people delegated upward! As I get stronger
here, I will be able to get meetings over faster, give
better direction, and refuse upward delegation.

Tool Kit: Action Minutes Save Time

Though you should always send an agenda in advance of the meetings you call, we recommend this added time-saver: Get attendees to
write their own *action minutes.* Using a flip chart or transparency, put
up the main agenda items in plain view as the meeting begins. As
agenda decisions are made, have someone enter the outcomes on
each. Responsible or concerned parties take their own notes from
those action minutes so that formal minutes don't need to be issued
later and no debate or uncertainty ensues. If people disagree, they
must speak now or "hold their peace" after the meeting. I watched
this technique in action at the annual planning meeting of a major
furniture manufacturer in Chicago. "Action Minutes" charts lined the
walls as the three-day meeting concluded. Before going home to their
various global locations, meeting members viewed those charts and
took notes on actions they had to carry out when they returned home.
Everyone had the same chance to return from the meeting, "singing
from the same song sheet."

An Illuminating Interview: Communicating Well on Priorities

Tom Sawyers is an R&D engineering planner for a large wireless communication company. He has a long history in aerospace and other
high-tech fields. Today, he has several bosses: the engineering director, the materials engineer, and one or more materials program managers, each running different product lines. Tom says:

> To solve priority disputes you need two things:
> 1. A clear sense of the bottom line as the "big guy" sees
>   it.
> 2. Absolute knowledge of your boundaries: How much
>   authority you have to say yes or no to unrealistic re-
>   quests.
>
> I always try to put myself in the requester's spot—have some
> understanding of his situation. If there's a gray area where
> we should bend to help him, we do it. But if I'm bending the
> rules, I copy relevant people by e-mail so they get a heads up
> and we get some safety.

Tom's View of Unreasonable People:

> If somebody pushes me hard, I push back. But I also have to know when to back off . . . that comes from "seasoned intuition." If people make an unreasonable demand, I take the time to quickly review how the system works. Sometimes people don't have a clue about lead times; that information is outside their realm. With a little investment of my time, they realize what is possible. Most people are reasonable, then, and we can be creative with solutions.

About Saying No:

> You have to do it honestly. You also have to know who the players are . . . who has clout, who will escalate . . . and often, you have to let them. Then you rely on the top dog trusting you.

If You Have to Elevate a Dispute:

> Mostly, you can elevate one level informally by e-mail without offending anyone. If the demand is an everyday thing with no lateral impacts, you can keep it on a peer level. If your adjoining departments can't or won't cooperate, you may have to elevate one level further.

About Rapid Priority Changes:

> In our business, changes don't come daily, they come by the minute. You can have a product due by the end of the month, and any minute the schedule can tighten by a full week. My director can meet me in the hallway and say: "I need a new panel by the end of the week." So I schedule to fit it in. Minutes later, my immediate boss tells me we have four or five new changes on current projects. We immediately redraw the schedule: We may go back to the director and show him that his new panel is now fourth, not first, on the list. We put the ball back in his court, and he is always reasonable about it.

About Vital Communication:

> We use software to update demand and schedule adjustments continually. An internal requester can look at it any time if he's uncomfortable with what we tell him. But most people take our point very quickly around here.

About Dealing With Manipulative Negotiators:

> My advice is: Don't do it alone. Do it on e-mail—copying the
> right people—or by speakerphone with everyone aware who
> is present. Do it face-to-face but with an associate or boss
> present.

About Trust and Priority Juggling:

> In our business, CEO's are in their 30s, less formal, less hier-
> archical. If you have a good technical education, then age,
> gender, and connections don't matter. You are trusted by
> what you can do consistently. You simply get on with it!

No Triumph: A Tragedy

Communication can fail if you don't ask the right question! At a major
East Coast bank, the mail room got a late-afternoon call from the secretary to the CEO, asking that an envelope be retrieved before the
day's mail went out. Her voice sounded so urgent that the mail room
manager sprang into action even though this "save" would involve
pulling his staff off all other tasks and delaying all the mail. By working
the whole team at high speed, he found the letter. It had cost them
eight man-hours, so he hoped it involved a large transaction.

Delivering the envelope to the top floor in triumph, the mail room
manager asked the secretary what type of "save" this had been so he
could thank and motivate the crew. "Oh," she answered, "it was an
invitation to a speaker for a company event, but the boss decided to
postpone the function."

The manager's face fell. It would have been better, he thought, to
have withdrawn or postponed the invitation, than to have incurred
eight man-hours of sweat for so small a result. The secretary could
have asked how long such a search would take. But she did not. The
mail room manager, knowing how much work it might take, could
have asked just how critical this was, and weighed the importance
against his crew's time. But both parties were blinded by the clout of
the CEO. Silence overruled common sense, wasted corporate resources, and deflated team morale. The manager left in silence. No
lesson was learned on the top floor.

Lessons Learned Here

When they hear an odd request, good customer service managers are
quick to ask:

What result are you looking for? We have many options for handling this. Some might prove faster and cheaper—and get you the same result.

Try asking that results question when a demand threatens priorities or escalates costs. As a team, formulate good questions that help you to hold your priorities and to avoid blind responses to customer demands.

Summary: Ten Communication Points to Ponder

1. *Make your priorities visible for your own sake as well as for others.*

2. *Impose a selective principle.* Only majors can bump a major.

3. *Never ignore interrupters.* Use the dot chart to highlight those clients who need a nonrandom channel. Negotiate new options with them.

4. *Don't feel obliged to deal with distress on the spot.* An appointment may serve both parties better.

5. *Manage priorities by making tough decisions on survivability—whether to do tasks.* Manage time by making mechanical decisions on scheduling—*when* to do tasks. Priority management is much more difficult than time management.

6. *Override the old axioms such as first things first and first come, first served.* Always question the need to satisfy early birds and squeaky wheels.

7. *Use three criteria: energy, access, and privacy to determine the best time to slot a task.* The earliest start time is not always the best.

8. *Follow six new standards for consistent priority management.*

- High risk and high value must win.
- Urgency breaks ties between two priorities of equal risk and value.
- Clout is secondary to risk and value.
- When *short-range* tasks attack *long-range* tasks, the one with the highest impact wins.
- Give the same scrutiny to prevention and reaction.
- Users pay for chronic misuse of emergency services.

9. *Tool Kit: Work-Worry-Warn Tool.* You'll estimate tasks with tough deadlines and provide early warning to requesters.

10. *Offer rules and tools, such as off-limit times during the day, timed agendas, and action minutes, to help your multiple bosses reduce meeting madness.*

3 "Just Say No": Not an Option

" **J** ust say no!" Nancy Reagan's anti-drug campaign taught children all over the United States that on some subjects, *no* was enough, no further explanations or excuses were required. That memorable campaign spawned wall signs that blared:

NO IS A COMPLETE SENTENCE!

AND

WHAT PART OF NO

DON'T YOU UNDERSTAND?

As an astute professional, however, you've learned that the word *no* falls harshly on the ears of bosses, colleagues, and customers. A flat *no* can damage relationships and stunt your career, creating resentments that follow you for years. Your flat refusal can mark you as rude, uncooperative, egotistical, even insubordinate. On the other hand, you cannot simply surrender to a barrage of daily requests whose practical, technical, or moral risks are evident to you.

Negotiate, Don't Capitulate

This fast, five-part approach will serve you better.

1. When the answer *should* be no, don't *say* no. It's too hard to prove you are performing a service when you are saying no. Requesters cannot hear your rationale while they are feeling denied. Instead, they focus on creating their own arguments and defenses.

2. Open, instead, with this remark: "I see a risk to you." Emphasize the risks your requester would face if you were to say yes. Better still, if you are face to face with the requester, show him the risk. Sketch something for him, something he can take away with him should he need to defend his returning empty-handed to disappointed

clients or bosses. Make sure he can see as well as hear about the risks.

3. Caution: don't mention the risks or inconvenience to you or your team. Requesters expect you to handle those yourself. Instead, show them risks that will impact on *them*.

4. If requesters complain, assure them that you are striving to protect them from blind risks.

5. Finally, for any risk you point out, you must offer an option. Better still, invite the person to join you in finding a lower-risk option.

Seven Requests You Cannot Say Yes To

As a caring professional, you'll sacrifice gladly for the common good; you will stretch yourself in an emergency. But when competing demands converge at once, you need a clear set of principles to guide your choices. At our seminars, when we ask attendees to list demands that deserve a *no,* we get the same kinds of answers, enthusiastically endorsed, even from dedicated workers. Most people feel the urge to say no to:

1. Random, trivial interruptions that threaten vital working time.

2. Emergencies arising from another's neglect, especially after warnings.

3. Manipulation by people trying to palm off work.

4. Personal favors—even if owed—that conflict with higher priorities in a tight time frame.

5. Demands that offend your moral or ethical convictions.

6. Short-term demands with long-term hidden risks.

7. Demands, even from "on high," that are technically infeasible.

Your Reaction

What would you add?

8. _____

9. _____

10. _____

Five Sample Scenarios

Let's consider some situations in which a savvy worker would need to point out risks to requesters:

1. Hal interrupts you with an urgent but low-impact item while you struggle with a high-impact project due today. You might open with:

> I'd like to help you, Hal . . . I'm on a major project with a tight deadline. If five to ten minutes will help, I can give you time at 10:30. Otherwise, I must suggest that you try . . . [*Offer alternate source.*]

Then, show Hal that your major project takes almost all of today's schedule. You show him that the 10:30 slot you are offering is the only time you have left.

> If that won't do, Hal, I can call you tomorrow.

Hal sees that there is nothing peremptory about your response. The schedule was set before he arrived. You are willing but unable to stop for him.

2. Despite your warnings about lead time, Ingrid misses her deadline for services in your department. She now shows up late, expecting you to clear the decks and put her first in a heavy day. You show her that other vital work has occupied her abandoned slots. You offer her a compromise slot, and you ask, *"What would it take for you to meet the next deadline?"* You may learn about a legitimate, chronic problem she faces. By focusing her on *next time,* you highlight what is still possible. Thus you avoid pushing her to defensive excuse making.

3. Jerry is to be temporarily assigned elsewhere. In the days before the change, you can't help noticing that he deliberately puts aside one hated task to palm off on his short-term replacement . . . you! You might say,

> Jerry, in the three days you'll be gone, I'm glad to stand in on the usual run of work, but I notice you're stacking up all the customer complaints as they come in. By the time I take over from you, some of these clients will be pretty frustrated. I'm worried.

Jerry may try to fob you off. You might need to press on:

> Please don't allow these cases to backlog. It would be tough for me to do triple the usual number of these cases. If you

leave me an unbalanced workload, I might have to decline helping. What can we do to avoid *that*?

4. You asked Kit to cover for you last Thanksgiving weekend, and you agreed to do the same for her next Memorial Day weekend. Now, just before Christmas, when you are planning a trip home, she surprises you by claiming her payback now. You remind her of the deal you made for May. Kit tells you an elaborate story to justify the change: She complains that you "owe" her and that Memorial Day was a poor swap for her to accept. To avoid being manipulated, you might say,

> Kit, I do sympathize, yet I must say no. We had a deal for May. I made commitments for Christmas. Because I value our friendship, I'm willing to renegotiate some holiday other than May, if you need a better swap. I can't manage Christmas with so little notice. If you check among the rest of the team you'll find that some of the unmarried folks are staying in town. Someone is bound to like the idea of double pay for covering Christmas. Why not ask around?

5. Your company has a rule against associates dating their supervisors, even when both parties are single. Your boss suspects a fellow supervisor of breaking this rule. Hearing that the couple frequent the same theater group in which you are a member, he asks you to report whether or not you see them together at forthcoming productions. This makes you uncomfortable. You might reply:

> While I like to say yes to any requests of yours, I feel uncomfortable with this. I would not want to act as an investigator in my free time, no matter who asked me. Please find another way to conduct your investigation. I'm not judging your right or need to do this—ask Human Resources about it—but I must decline.

Consider Your Own Applications

Think about some dilemmas that require a caring no from you. Try scripting your best responses to your most common dilemmas. Design some rational responses before you need them. Map out illustrations you might use to warn requesters of blind risks they are incurring. With this scripting and sketching done, you'll be in better shape to react calmly when the need arises. Don't wait until the dispute arises to construct your defenses. When you're surprised or upset, it's doubly difficult to say no. Here's another case in point.

Case 6. Assigned Too Late

Presented by Lorenzo Rios, a senior ad designer for a retail chain.

My boss is infamous for sitting on work, delivering it to us at the last minute, then blaming us if we cannot finish it by deadline. Worse, he goes home on time each night, and spends a lot of Saturdays golfing with the top brass, while we sweat out the unpaid overtime to make his deadlines. He never shares credit or thanks with any associates. I want to say no, but I'm sure he would retaliate at review time.

First Pass: Written Solutions From Seminar Colleagues

1. Try a tickler file with days 1–31 for each month. Then remind the boss of the date and time the work will be due. If the boss continues to ignore warnings and you know you are doing your best, I would consider leaving.

2. Keep a log showing work assignments and completion dates. This is your proof that work is assigned late in a chronic pattern.

3. Discuss your resentment frankly. Escalate if you get no satisfaction.

4. For regularly scheduled work (meetings, presentations) for which your managers owe you data, post a two-column chart showing work due and the due dates on the left column, and data received on the right column. This will serve as a gentle visual reminder before the fact: proactive rather than reactive.

5. When work is handed to you, inform the person that you doubt it can be completed by its deadline. Suggest that some of the work must be shared among several workers to meet the deadline.

Your Reaction: What Advice Would You Endorse or Add?

_____

_____

_____

_____

_____

Second Thoughts Expressed in Group Discussion

1. *About tickler files in general.* With today's trend toward the paperless office, tickler files are bowing to graphic schedules on shared computer screens, flagged to remind bosses and indeed all team members of vital deadlines. Even with a wall chart schedule, Lorenzo could control work with a calendar, and keep only one set of files instead of both subject files and tickler files. The risk with tickler files is that someone must access that file whenever Lorenzo is away. But a shared wall or computer calendar with flagged reminders warns everyone, visibly and continuously, of important deadlines. As for leaving the department, it's a bit early to think of that. Never leave until all avenues of negotiation have been exhausted.

2. *Sure, log incoming work, but always include an estimate of lead times needed to complete the work.* Even with hard-to-estimate work, a collection of log sheets will build you a pretty good indicator of standard times for different types of work, and this may stimulate better team performance next time. Lesson: Don't use your logs as an accusation; use them to build standard procedures and lead times.

3. *Escalate?* Not yet! Start by discussing task needs, not your resentments. Escalating has two drawbacks: It raises the cost per hour of fixing the problem, and it can make you seem to be a troublemaker—especially in a dispute with only two witnesses, one of whom outranks you! Escalate only after all other avenues have been explored.

4. *Create a two-column chart showing due dates and obligations fulfilled.* This proactive approach looks practical and easy for Lorenzo.

5. *Express doubts early, ask for help.* Good, but don't wait until work is handed to you to negotiate. As much as possible, use a proactive menu or map of work types and the lead times necessary to fulfill them. Then insist on enough lead time. Hiring extra help is only one of several possible choices. Consider these options, starting with the most obvious:

- You can negotiate to extend the deadline into the future.
- You can negotiate for more help.
- You can negotiate to shrink the scope of the project.
- You can negotiate to reduce the level of perfection/detail asked. You can probably dream up more options, but these are the essentials. You reduce resentments

when you teach yourself and others that options abound.

Consensus Recommendations

Develop and share standard lead-time data if you hope to curtail unrealistic last-minute assignments. By the time an assignment is made, it is too late to negotiate. As for bosses sharing credit or publicizing your accomplishments, the best of them do this quite naturally. They know it motivates. But unless you signed some agreement that gives you ownership of your intellectual property, every good thing you do for your company is theirs, and they have no obligation to credit you. Relax about this. More than half the bosses in your life will credit you, but some won't. Choose any attitude other than resentment. Philosophers say that resentment corrodes its container long before it gets the attention of the guilty.

Asserting Yourself Without Hurting Yourself

Do anything you can to quiet your inner resentments. The hurt feelings expressed by Lorenzo in Case 6 might drive him to attack or vilify his boss in an unguarded moment. This can be damaging or fatal to any career. Victimized feelings show up in helpless language. Learn to curtail it, even when talking to yourself.

Victim Vocabulary: Six Things Never to Say

I can't: "I can't get this done on such short notice."
I'm sorry: "I'm sorry, but company policy forbids my doing this."
I wish you: "I wish you had brought this to me sooner."
If only you: "If only you had warned us this was coming."
You always: "You always expect me to drop everything for you."
You never: "You never consider the inconvenience to others."

These are unhelpful, for obvious reasons. Some statements make the speaker sound helpless or inadequate, tempting angry requesters to retaliate:

You can't? Then let's find someone who can!

If your statements seem to accuse the requester, you may trigger hostile responses. Replace each of the weak-kneed statements above with more powerful, yet less provocative, comments.

Six Things to Say Instead

I can do this for you if some conditions are met . . .

Let me point out something to help you avoid a risk . . .

To do this, I would need from you . . .

Much as I want to help you, here's a risk that might negate all the benefits you are seeking . . .

Let me point out a pattern I'm seeing . . . a pattern of last-minute assignments that put your work at risk . . .

Allow me to show you the record on this. Delays are reducing your chance of getting work done to standard . . .

To help you out here, I'd need a new standard procedure and a new queuing order that justifies bumping scheduled tasks, including some of yours . . .

Case 7. Palmed-Off Job?

Presented by Mark Bauer, an engineering estimator.

How do I refuse a high-risk estimating job (no previous model or precedent) that I know is the boss's responsibility, not mine? I know what types of work are pegged for different levels of manager here, and I don't like this high-cost work palmed off on me. Unlike my boss, I lack the budget and clout to call on outside consulting services and internal data sources required to build a new estimating model.

First Pass: Written Solutions From Seminar Colleagues

1. Don't say a flat no. Be diplomatic. Explain your time pressures or point out technical and political risks that make this job dangerous.

2. Ask what steps the boss takes, or has taken, to guarantee accuracy with this type of estimate. Ask for the best advice on how you can handle it. Ask for training or a break-in period with a supervisor. I don't see how the boss can refuse this. It's delegation!

3. Sit down and run the first attempt in tandem with the boss so she doesn't evade doing it. Get her to steer you away from the problems you would face in trying it alone. Then be glad when you've added a superior skill level to your repertoire.

Your Reaction: What Advice Would You Endorse or Add?

_____

_____

_____

_____

_____

Second Thoughts Expressed in Group Discussion

1. *Diplomacy is not the only requirement here, or even the main one.* It is every manager's right to delegate any type of work, except discipline and decision making. The boss can ask any appropriate subordinate to do legwork, research, or any standard operation necessary to get a project done. As soon as a senior manager has made a once-risky operation less risky, that operation can and should be delegated. With this in mind, you are correct to point out time conflicts and show the risks of delaying other tasks so that your manager can make a sensible decision about delegating to you. But reconsider telling your boss that delegation is out of bounds. Delegation means, literally, that a senior releases some of her work downward.

2. *Get the boss's help with the risks.* Good reply. From the boss's answers, you can easily create a template on step-by-step handling of new estimates, rules, or calculations for gaining accuracy, or political advice on questions to ask. You can also negotiate a break-in period during which monitoring and error-correction are offered. Workers can expect bosses to provide training as a central part of delegation. Your boss may intend to include this when she assigns this work to you.

3. *Ask for a tandem first attempt.* This is another good option, seeking more hands-on help from the boss. Ask for it, but never hint that the boss is trying to evade work. If you work in a department where high-risk estimating is needed, to earn promotion, you'll have to get experience with this at some time.

Consensus Recommendations

Use difficult new assignments as a stepping stone to promotion and a chance at more exciting work. It's all right to reveal your nervousness if it is seen as appropriate humility. Take all the steps you need to learn correctly and reduce risks on your first try. Express your delight in being trusted with higher-level work. Negotiate a training and break-in period. Once into the task, you might even inquire about added rewards (pay and status hikes) as you progress from probation to full takeover of the work. Sure, the company should expect to save money in moving the task down a step, but they *may* not insist on keeping 100 percent of the savings. If you feel confident, go after your share.

When You Must Say No on Moral Grounds

Many people find it easiest to say no when a request conflicts clearly with their moral or ethical convictions. While great books and movies have been based on the courage shown in the face of moral dilemmas, many managers in business and government have told me that they struggle more for clarity than for courage in specific situations. Those who have drawn clear boundaries of conscience around certain issues can say no from a clear imperative. The more mature they are, the more choices they have for couching that *no* in firm but nonoffensive terms. Watch how the audience responds to the next case and you'll see that clarity is not so easy to achieve and that courage sometimes speaks too soon.

Case 8. A Script Too Rosy

Presented by Neal Kennedy, a customer service representative in information services.

While most department heads in my company are dedicated, caring, and honest, I have one supervisor who asks us to hedge, equivocate, and paint unduly rosy pictures for customers. Later, when we must break promises, we are first in line for attack by angry and disappointed customers. When I was new here, I believed what supervisors told me. Now, I am skeptical: I want to say no to these shortsighted, rosy "scripts," but most of my colleagues, fearful for their jobs, bow to this supervisor. I'm not a one-man moral police force, but this deceit offends me to the point where I feel like quitting or blowing the whistle!

First Pass: Written Solutions From Seminar Colleagues

1. Before quitting, calculate the ratio of promises that fail against those that pan out. What is your industry average on

performance? Can you prove comparable poor performance by your company, or dishonorable intentions on any supervisor's part? If not, be careful of accusing people. Very few companies can guarantee every single promise. But good companies do have programs for making things right with their few disappointed customers: rain checks, price breaks for waiting, that sort of incentive. Are you being puritanical in your views?

2. If you want to complain to the supervisor, go ahead. But don't decide that you're the only honest person in your outfit. Poll some co-workers. They may not be as fearful as you think; instead, they may agree with the supervisor's approach.

3. You don't mention having discussed this with the supervisor. Have you simply made up your mind without asking tactful questions?

4. If you're describing a pattern or trend, your company must be bleeding customers. Is it? Is business declining? Then you could risk going over your case to the powers that be. Take your chances, but don't be wrong or careless with your figures.

Your Reaction: What Advice Would You Endorse or Add?

_____

_____

_____

_____

_____

Second Thoughts Expressed in Group Discussion

All answers are sensible, suggesting that you check your facts and widen your perspective. Then you might venture some communication risks rather than go on stewing. Neal blurted out his discontent at the seminar with more passion than perspective. The advice he got from fellow attendees was also kinder in tone than it now appears on the page. Neal was impressed enough at their advice to hang out with some of these people later in the day. He went home more comfortable with getting his facts together and proposing better scripts to his boss.

Consensus Recommendations

"To thine own self be true" is still good advice. It may or may not win you friends in high places, but it might keep you off the psychiatrist's couch. Repositioning your boundaries should be a personal choice, worthy of serious thinking in quiet hours.

Enhance Your Perspective With Added Options

Here are two added options to help you reduce moral frustrations at work.

1. If you don't like a client service script given you by the company, try writing three or four new scripts, varying in frankness and detail; then negotiate with the company to test these more candid scripts with customers. Keep good numbers on responses. You may prove that candor works best . . . or perhaps not.

2. Get outside opinions. Join a professional group for customer service reps; attend meetings where you can discuss best practices and problem solving to help your company develop more options. In the safety of a professional group, you can develop a more mature perspective to your own thinking without revealing naïveté or compromising your integrity.

Reduce Rudeness and Righteous Indignation

In the case just concluded, the upset customer service rep could have used the formula suggested at the start of this chapter: Don't say no . . . show risk. When you do show a risk, show an option.

Let this two-part formula work for you when *no* is the sensible answer.

How to Calm Distraught Customers

When customers are disappointed, when your company's policy appears to say no to their needs, you use a caring manner and a reliable script. You offer the customer understanding, sympathy, satisfaction, and direction—*not* an argument. Therefore, you say things like: *"I can certainly understand your viewpoint . . ."* not *"I see that you're upset!"* Avoid describing a person's emotions to him unless you are a psychiatrist, and even then, you'd do it sparingly.

If a person rants on uncontrollably, you might say:

"Yes, I've got that. Yes, I understand." Or, "Let me get this correctly: You say that . . ."

(You repeat without embellishments or judgments. You cite facts and events only.)

How to Respond With Compassion

One medical secretary assists a chief of oncology at a major hospital. Often, she is first in line to take phone complaints from patients' families. People get upset when loved ones are hospitalized, especially if the news is bad. Sometimes their fear, uncertainty, and sense of helplessness erode their natural good manners. When a hysterical caller seethes about some disadvantage, real or imagined, suffered by his loved one, this secretary says:

I do sympathize with the distress you're having. Tell me what happened. . . . And then what happened? Yes. I see.

As the caller talks, she offers empathy, not defenses or apologies. If the caller goes on for too long, the secretary may say:

It's natural to have a lot of questions at a time like this. You've mentioned many important items to me, and I've written them down. Now that we know all the items you want us to consider, let's decide which items are most important to you . . . Let's prioritize and we'll work on those first.

This helps the caller calm down. It gets him to focus on the future. Note what the secretary avoided saying. She deliberately avoided: *"I can't help unless you calm down."* Or, *"Please calm down . . ."* The first sentence would make her sound incapable; the second would shame or blame the caller, risking an angry escalation.

Similarly, a prison social worker offers these suggestions for dealing with irate clients. She often faces abuse and profanity from distressed people. She replies to such torrents with maximum detachment and kindness:

Do you want me to include this last part? I'm taking this down for the official record. Let's make sure it represents you well on paper.

At those words, her callers often apologize for exploding. This woman is not a saint: she is practical enough to realize that these clients will maintain contact over a long period of time. There must be no residual anger or shame to contaminate future transactions. She considers it vital to let callers feel whatever they are feeling and to express it. But she does not take responsibility for causing other people's feelings. That's why she can express understanding without becoming vulnerable herself. Before closing such an encounter, she takes a moment to review:

> Let's just review where we are. When you called you had a concern about . . . Now, you want us to arrange . . . I'll research your request before the (committee, authority, decision maker) and you'll hear from me by 4:00 today (noon Tuesday or whatever).

She usually closes the call with:

> And thank you for working with me on this. Do you think we did well together?

Often, the distraught caller is able to sign off with thanks.

By going patiently through this process, she helps clients withdraw from the past (their anger), move into the present (your problem is now recorded), and then focus on the future (solution by noon Tuesday).

Liberate Yourself From Other People's Fear

One of the most freeing thoughts you can hold is the view that most people's bad behavior arises from fear. Your job as a professional is to reduce that fear and move people forward. Whatever the subject, each ring of your phone, each walk-in interruption is a chance for you and another person to make progress together and emerge better than when you started. Many great customer service people have told me that bringing a caller to a better place has motivated their entire service career.

An Illuminating Interview: On Hidden Agendas

The most dangerous no is the one you say to a boss with a strong hidden agenda. I got this story from a food service manager at a big high school in a southwestern town. Let's call her Carol.

Not all bad behavior arises from personality. Some people have nice little rackets going, and they attack whoever catches them at it. As a subordinate in these situations, you need courage and a network in order to fight back. I'm active in the union and have made many friends in management after serving in several schools over the past twenty-five years.

Carol is proud of her record for saving money and plowing it back into food service for the benefit of the kids. Going over her profit and loss statement one month, she saw a very high charge for "other services"—charges allocated across all schools. She questioned her direct boss. Only with reluctance did the boss reveal the details. It turned out that the big expense was for large write-on wall calendars distributed to all school departments a month earlier. Examining the paperwork, Carol saw that the calendars had come through this boss's daughter, who had outsold all her classmates in a fund-raising project. There were other "charitable donations" on the statement, making up the high total.

Retaliation for Carol's persistence was not long in coming.

On a regular basis, school food staffers prepare popular snacks (aside from the formal lunch program). The kids pay for these afternoon treats; the food services make a "profit," which is then used for food service equipment or upgrades that benefit the kids. When Carol's team made a very large profit that season, this boss decided to allocate half of the savings to the school's ailing sports program. Carol argued that this countermanded district policy and would demotivate the food service staff. The boss was adamant. Carol felt obliged to take her protest to the superintendent of schools, but not directly. She tried through her network, talking with the superintendent's secretary and mentioning only her anxiety to prevent the appearance of fraud.

I had to know whom to ask and how to say it in ways that cited error or appearances rather than intent to defraud. I did not mention nor condemn that boss. I checked with my other bosses, in principle only, to get their opinions on strict allocation of funds. I had good backup in place. Within days an announcement came out, reminding all schools that funds raised by the efforts of any single entity were to be plowed into improvements for that entity, and could not be drawn on by others.

Saying no and making it stick took vigilance and energy, but winning that round helped to reignite Carol's team. Carol is not a favorite with this particular boss, but her essential goodwill and discretion have won support from other senior managers and kept the lid on a problem that could have escalated badly.

Triumphs and Turnarounds:
The Telecommunications Industry

Perhaps the hardest no is the one you say to a once-in-a-lifetime offer. Latasha K., an engineer in the telecommunications industry, told us this story. For years, she had struggled to gain legitimacy among her male peers and her several old-line bosses. She was finally offered a hotly contested job. At the time, her personal life was turbulent. Her child suffered a health crisis after a long bout with a chronic illness. Her husband, himself exhausted from the long siege, had abandoned the family. The promotion would have offered more money but longer hours and travel. Latasha gave it careful consideration, prayed over it, and decided she could not cope with her life situation and manage the new job at the same time. Her co-workers predicted that her turndown now would cut her chances of future promotion. She did not agree. She checked with her other bosses; they were split on how the "big guy" would react. She went to her main boss with this forthright statement:

> Although I am grateful for the offer, I need to stay in my current position where I know I can get excellent results for the company and be there for my child, too. If the baby's health improves, I know that my track record will open up some new opportunities for me, here or elsewhere. I cannot allow anxiety to push me into this job at the wrong moment. It wouldn't be best for you, the team, or me. I believe this is not the first nor the last promotion I will be offered.

Her boss was surprised for a moment, then impressed with her convictions. Sadly, she told us, her child did not survive that crisis. She testified at the seminar that she'd had two promotions since that sacrifice, and that she would always remain proud of herself for making a judgment that turned out best for her and her child at a moment of great meaning in her life.

Summary: "Just Say No": Not an Option

1. *Don't just say no.* Show risks and offer options graphically.
2. *Determine which requests you can't say yes to.*
3. *Create some warning scripts before the need for no arises.*
4. *Negotiate to get help, shrink scope, extend deadlines, or reduce detail levels so you can still say yes.*

4. *Avoid "victim vocabulary": . . . I can't . . . you never . . . why?*

5. *Treat irate customers as very important "bosses."*

6. *Avoid judging others' motives without evidence.*

7. *Submit improved versions of corporate scripts that dismay you.*

8. *Join professional groups for safer perspectives on which requests to accept and which to dispute or decline.*

9. *You can often get what you need, keeping others just honest enough to achieve that, without "calling the morality cops."*

10. *Believe that having earned promotion once, you can earn it again.* Be at peace when you must say no to a career offer.

However nicely you do it, pointing out risks will lead inevitably to conflicts with the more self-willed among your contacts. We'll tackle that next.

4 Conflict Survival School

J ust let one person mention "personality conflicts" at a seminar, and the whole room sits up straight! Whether participants are senior managers, secretaries, or technicians, they all debate with vigor on this subject. Of course, any multiple-demand job site is a veritable petri dish for incubating conflicts. In any situation where many contenders compete for shrinking resources, you'll see conflict bloom in living color. Whether it's the last helicopter leaving the embassy rooftop, or the last call for graphics before the annual meeting, you'll witness similar behavior from desperate refugees and determined executives.

To succeed at managing multiple bosses, you'll need to develop clear-headed, deliberate detachment. Start making conflict management your specialty. Notice and enjoy your successes at sorting out priorities with minimum friction. For this you'll need two things: a wholesome disinterest in personality conflicts and a set of tools.

First, Quit Your Role as Volunteer Therapist

Everyone's favorite pastime at work seems to be practicing psychiatry without a license. Face it—no matter how experienced and sophisticated you are, no matter how smoothly diplomatic, you cannot bring about change in another adult's personality. If you cannot change it, why focus on it? If you yearn to change another, and if you are caught trying, the person with the unlovely personality trait clings to it more tightly and counts you as an enemy.

Can you really give up the wish to change other people? Child care experts tell us that personalities are formed at an early age. Certainly by our seventh year, human personalities are essentially built. Traits may mature, or they may mellow like good wine or strong cheese, but drastic changes occur only through traumatic events. Do you really want to be someone's trauma? To move toward change, people must see a causal link between their behavior and some ensuing harsh consequences. But people tend to blame outside events, enemies, or fate for painful consequences. Even when we see that our behavior is causing us grief, we are hesitant to change wholesale. We're more likely to experiment with small, easy adjustments at first. If better outcomes ensue, a person may gradually shift attitudes, sometimes without realizing it. Change is a slow process; it's always an inside job. Therefore, to criticize others, to nag them about changing their deeply or unconsciously held traits, can hardly be expected to succeed quickly, if at all. Yet some people stubbornly persist.

Case 9. "Remote" Controller

Presented by Quentin Murray, an engineer in telecommunications.

I have four bosses. Three are normal human beings: The fourth is quiet, remote, and uncommunicative. I can't tell how I stand with him since he is the same ultra-controlled self whether I do something fabulous or something modest on his projects. He communicates only by e-mail; any face-to-face stuff is as brief as he can make it. He's never said "please" or "thanks" or "good job" to anyone yet. I don't know how to break through his shell.

First Pass: Written Solutions From Seminar Colleagues

1. If you have regular meetings with the other bosses, offer to set up similar regular meetings with him, just for balance and fairness. If he's not interested, relax. It's OK to keep things strictly business if that seems to make him comfortable.

2. Draw this person into friendly conversation. Avoid strictly personal stuff, but try the usual: sports, weather, local entertainment, holidays, vacations, that sort of thing. Tell him a little about your hobbies and interests, and sound him out about his. Then listen appreciatively. Take it slow.

3. Tell this person you are worried and want to create a better working relationship; that you'd like a one-on-one occasionally to be sure he is getting all that he needs from you.

4. Let this boss know the various ways you use to keep the others informed. Ask which method this manager prefers, and whether he is satisfied with the service you provide. Some people want their relationships and reports to be formal and written; others use casual verbal exchanges. Perhaps you need constant reassurance, while this boss is merely showing that you are trusted. Go with whatever level this person seems to need. You could even be grateful that one of your bosses makes himself scarce—you'll have more time to yourself!

Your Reaction: What Advice Would You Endorse or Add?

_____

_____

_____

_____

_____

Second Thoughts Expressed in Group Discussion

1. *Offer to set up regular meetings as you do for others.* Sure, you can offer, but don't be surprised if he declines. Just relax and get on with it.

2. *Draw him out.* You can always say more about yourself, but don't probe for more information about him. And don't be offended if your chatter makes him irritable. He has demonstrated that chat is not his style. Since he is remote with everyone, it's got nothing to do with you. Pressure may push him further away.

3. *Express your worry.* If you risk doing this, make sure it's weeks before your performance review. Use this context: *"Boss, it's hard to forecast how I'm doing as we approach my performance review. Anything I should be doing differently to meet your requirements?"* Don't complain about his style; he probably cannot change. If he's satisfied with your performance, then let it go.

4. *Ask what he prefers and be satisfied.* Uncongenial people often have other virtues: They let you use your head. Don't try to cuddle up to this guy.

Consensus Recommendations

Many people agree that the most dangerous position you can take is one of probing disapproval of any boss, especially in the hearing of his management colleagues. Awaiting the right moment to complain or perform "brain surgery" on your boss, you make yourself miserable and jumpy. Learn to "detach"—to care less about other people's motives and foibles. When you stop wanting to change people, you conserve amazing amounts of energy with which to perfect your own job!

Excise the Term "Personality Conflict" From Your Vocabulary

You may be more comfortable with one personality style than another, but be careful. Not only should you avoid seeking to change another adult's personality, but you must consciously sidestep three other traps:

1. Never admit to having a *personality conflict* with another person. If bosses hear you criticizing a co-worker or fellow boss, they are likely to think "it takes two" to make a disagreement. Just eliminate that expression from your conversation!

2. Don't allow anyone to accuse you of having a personality conflict with another.

3. Be equally loath to advise people on their personality conflicts. Attest that you have no license for it.

Admit That Most Conflicts Are About Power

The license you do have—in fact, all workers have it—is the license to reduce conflicts by redistributing *powers*, not by changing *personalities*. To solve any conflict, you can use your experience, common sense, goodwill, and diplomacy to bring about change because you and another person are simply seeking to redistribute an external entity: POWER. It may be the power to do something or not to do it, the power to share work or not to share it, to redistribute credit, rewards, space, tasks—or not to do so. You must believe firmly that each party in a conflict has the power to do good, to improve situations, and to create options.

- You need never use the word *power* if you think it will scare people.
- You need only define what *ability, facility, data, easement, access,* or *help* you need, and you can invite others to do likewise. You'll be working to redistribute *power* without using its name.

Test Your Detachment on This Scenario

Liberated from wanting to change others, how could you act helpfully in the following situation?

Jennifer, a friend and colleague, comes to you, complaining:

I have a personality conflict with George.

If you believe you have a license to change personalities, you may jump in with advice. However, if you believe personalities cannot or should not be changed except by the owner, you might respond with something akin to this:

> It's troubling to hear that, Jennifer, because I believe that personalities are impossible to change from outside. Personalities are so interior, so private, often so fragile, that we struggle to protect ours from outside probes or criticism.

You might let that thought penetrate. You could then continue with a suggestion like this:

> How about looking at this conflict in a different way? What if you stop thinking about it as a personality conflict and view it as a power conflict? Since the power to do things in this company is an external reality, you could ask what powers you and George are conflicting over. Are those powers really so limited that only one of you can use them? Or can they be manipulated, shared, multiplied, or redivided by you, by George, or by others?

This way of thinking may surprise Jennifer. In fact, she may return stubbornly to the subject of George's personality defects, wanting to convince you of his apparent egotism, lack of sensitivity, dishonesty, or whatever she judges in him. Be patient. Detachment is foreign to many people. Adhere to your point, quietly. Invite the complainer to consider once more:

> What power are you and George conflicting over? The power to supervise people? To get budget for a project? To change priorities? The power to use equipment? To talk directly to a client? To solve problems in a specific way? If you can get clear on that, you can solve it, with or without my help—and without diagnosing personality disorders.

Help Jennifer to externalize the problem. You may want to conclude this way:

> Whatever power you are conflicting over you may have a license to increase, decrease, or reapportion. But I have no license to practice psychiatry on either of you . . . and I believe that you and George can rearrange power between you without my help. Strictly avoid judging personalities or motives. Just ask for the behavior you need. If you picture someone as egotistical, insensitive, or dishonest, you decrease

your own willingness to negotiate. Your hidden disapproval comes across to the other person, triggering his need to deny or counterattack.

Today's detached approach to problem solving comes as a surprising relief to many workers, managers, and executives. Not so long ago, well-meaning, paternalistic companies fostered supervision as a form of parenting and employment as a form of dependency— building dysfunctional families at work. If people indulge in speculating on the motives of others, mean-spirited compulsions can run to the point of obsession until all the parties get hauled before Human Resources or EAP professionals for damage control.

Reduce Role Ambiguities

Often, what passes for personality conflict is simply confusion over being assigned unclear responsibilities with inadequate authority. That could have triggered the Jennifer–George conflict. It certainly operates in the situation that follows: A worker has multiple bosses, but she's the last to know!

Case 10. Ambiguous Arrangements

Presented by Richard Cruz, a senior medical researcher.

We operate as a team around here. But a junior researcher resents and discards my suggestions and corrections. She persists in doing things her way; her work often comes back to me with my boss's request for an upgrade. "Handle this personally," he asks, so I correct the work. When I try to coach this junior, she gets defensive. I've complained to the boss about the irrationality of this arrangement. He just says: "We're all a team here. She's still learning. You're senior to her, so handle it. Don't involve me." "She makes me mad," says Richard, "but the boss makes me even madder!"

First Pass: Written Solutions From Seminar Colleagues

1. I would tell her: "I am your supervisor. We have standards to maintain, and your success depends on your cooperation. I'll make the effort: You must meet me halfway."

2. Make allowances for newcomers. Is there a standard "break-in" time? Probe her background, fill in any training gaps, but name a deadline for compliance with quality standards.

3. Confront her with the evidence. Ask her how she plans to achieve the quality level required. Does she lack training? Access to any resources? Warn her that a reputation for sloppy work would kill most careers, but it is especially fatal in research. Give her an ultimatum. You need a written commitment from her, or else you cannot save her job.

4. Have the boss clarify to her in writing that you supervise her. Otherwise, you should opt out of vague "teamwork" arrangements that force you to supervise without clear authority. If you don't officially supervise her, remind the boss that he does!

Your Reaction: What Advice Would You Endorse or Add?

_____

_____

_____

_____

_____

Second Thoughts Expressed in Group Discussion

1. *Give her an ultimatum.* Do so if you *are* officially her supervisor. Otherwise, the trouble between you is hardly surprising.

2. *Make allowances.* Most of us would admit that new employees need a break-in period. But often, researchers, programmers, and other specialty workers are hired, not as trainees, but as experts, fully accredited in the area they are researching. What was the case here? And what training or break-in facilities are made available to incoming workers? It cannot be left to luck.

3. *Ask for her plan to upgrade quality.* This is a good, firm technique to be administered by anyone who does supervise or coach with authorization. If you are only a more senior colleague, however, and the employee has not been advised that you will coach her, you may be seen as a busybody, intruding between her and the boss.

4. *Get it in writing.* You're either a supervisor or an authorized coach. The written document should specify the duties and powers of each role. Unofficial and unannounced supervision hardly ever succeeds. Draft something, discuss it with a trusted party, then get the boss to sign it. If this worker

now has multiple bosses (your boss and you), have the decency to make it plain.

Consensus Recommendations

More personality conflicts arise from vague authority than from any other cause. Once you make rights and obligations clear, many so-called conflicts evaporate.

If you, like Richard's junior researcher, seem to have unofficial bosses, go to the senior people who hired you and get them to draw a clear organizational chart showing all persons to whom you are answerable.

Negotiate Irrational Workloads From Multi-Bosses

Your multidemand stresses can go from bad to worse if your senior managers assign work inequitably or settle your peer concerns in arbitrary fashion. Better to settle peer issues first, then get multi-boss approval on the plan. But many people go to the mountain without climbing the hill first. Witness this in the next case:

Case 11. Task Load Inequities

Presented by Stacy Mengburg, programmer at a software house.

I struggle with a mammoth project load. The faster I go, the more my three bosses heap on me. When I try to complain, they remind me I am their best programmer; they flatter me about the superior quality of my work. I suggested to one boss (the worst offender) that his form of loading is unfair—that my peers in the department have time to laze and kid around while I struggle. That set him off! He drew himself up to his full height and said: *"Stacy, you do not see the big picture and you are not in a position to judge the equity of my decisions."* How can I be expected to deal with a boss like that?

First Pass: Written Solutions From Seminar Colleagues

1. Shop around for another department where things are done fairly. It's hard to change situations in which all other members have settled in snugly while one workhorse is miserable. This status quo is likely to persist.

2. How effectively—if at all—have you asked peers for help with your load before you escalate to your bosses? Peo-

ple are often willing to help, but most will wait to be asked. As for this stuffy boss, the next time he tells you that you don't see the big picture, ask him to show it to you. If you *are* their best programmer, you need to understand the overall plan, absolutely.

3. Beware labeling your peers as lazy and your boss as unfair. It's hard to get multiple loads done while harboring ill will. Instead, try asking for help on limited, well-defined tasks. Is it possible that your pride made you accept undue loads in the past, or that your perfectionism made you turn help away when it was offered? If so, start again with a clean slate.

4. You mention one unsympathetic boss. Do you have better credibility with the others? Start negotiating with the two reasonable bosses. If they value your work, they may help you with the third man. You have not yet begun to fight. At least begin to divide the workloads into categories (levels of difficulty); decide which pieces you should be handling at your experience level, and which tasks could be handled by others. Your written recommendation, given to your three bosses, should help them decide which work goes where. With their endorsement, you might cross-train and upgrade performance skills among your peers, making for greater depth in the department and ways to spread work around.

Your Reaction: What Advice Would You Endorse or Add?

_____

_____

_____

_____

_____

Second Thoughts From Seminar Teams and Speaker

1. *Job hunt.* If you do shop around, don't mention complaints about your bosses or peers. Otherwise, some will assume you are the troublemaker, fair or not.

2. *Seek lateral help.* Sure, but no one gives something for nothing. What can you offer in trade for help from colleagues? Don't reject this question: negotiation means both sides give to get. Yes. Ask your boss #3 to share his big picture. Or you sketch out your view of things, and get him to confirm.

3. *Stop judging, and start asking.* It's a common trap to become isolated behind a huge workload, refusing to ask for help. Think back over recent weeks: did people offer to help, and did you turn them down? Many complainers sheepishly admit they have turned away help. Do that just once and you find yourself working alone.

4. *Map out load division, and get approval.* This good suggestion ties in with our enthusiasm for graphic messages. If you chart out the work as responder "4" suggests, you make your request objective and visual. You won't be seen as begging for relief: you'll be laying out a problem and offering team solutions. Recruit the two reasonable bosses to help you cement the outcome with the third.

Team Decision Making Reduces Conflict

Healthy companies find that the workers themselves have very keen insights into the risks in the team's workloads.

- When a Bank of America credit card team disputed an imposed load-sharing plan, the team members themselves charted and negotiated a work-sharing plan that was far more equitable—and far more sensitive to the bank's risks—than their bosses could have imagined. They were credited with good strategy, and their work plan was adopted. There's no greater motivator than having your proposals endorsed and enacted.
- At Delco's plant in Kokomo, Indiana, purchasing secretaries set up a program to allow people from the production line to work in the office: they gained understanding about one another's needs and priorities, reducing conflicts that used to threaten productivity. Management was delighted with this initiative.
- At NFO, an Ohio-based consumer research house, people from MIS and customer service took up temporary residence in each other's units to gain understanding of long-term conflicting needs and priorities. Better teamwork resulted; so called personality clashes melted; and management applauded and rewarded the effort.

But old habits die hard. Elsewhere, squabbling workers fear negotiating with peers. Instead, they call on senior managers to settle conflicts, thus delaying the acquisition of negotiating skills and perpetuating their own dependency. Then, they complain if management hatches a solution that burdens them further.

What Blocks You From Taking Initiative?

Multi-boss workers, heavily loaded, tend to squabble about priorities and task loads for two reasons:

1. They are not clued into management's overarching goals. They may lack a solid rationale for knowing how all jobs are meant to fit together.
2. They don't know what standards their conflicting tasks must meet, so they are unsure what quality level is required for each task.

"Why do senior managers hide the big picture from us?" you may ask. "Don't they see that conflicts will arise out of our imposed ignorance?"

Specialists, technicians, mid-level managers, and executive assistants often complain that they feel powerless in the face of rising demands, that their input is not welcomed, their anxieties cannot be heard . . . they're not even sure who initiates significant workloads. Too often, their opinion is sought only at late stages of decision-making when all but the tiniest details are set in stone. On workers' behalf, we've asked senior managers to tell us *why* they decide things unilaterally, discouraging early employee input, yet at the same time paying lip service to "empowerment."

We put these questions to top government managers. Here's how the senior officials replied, with remarkable candor, in written responses:

How Do Bosses Justify Blocking Worker Input?

- We don't want negative early feedback. It slows us down.
- We fear unilateral worker actions. They'll take off with it, leaving me and themselves shorter intervals for planning and adjusting.
- We want to shield subordinates from politics.
- We fear their reactions—the embarrassment of justifying our decisions and the time needed to correct their overreactions.
- We don't want to lose our own "fun" jobs too early, so we delegate only at the last minute and under duress.
- We want to "protect" subordinates from the consequences of hasty actions or leaked information.

What Would It Take to Open Up Earlier Participation?

- More technology is forcing technicians' earlier involvement. Top management simply cannot legislate without the techies.

- Accelerated change: Doing more with less means taking more input from lower levels, right from the start.

What Are You Doing Currently to Involve All Levels?

- We're creating joint signaling systems to avoid unilateral surprises.
- We inform people on the broad range of resources they can tap into—menus of benefits, job postings, more open forums on plans.
- We bring in professional and technical training so people have more career choices open to them.
- While we feel obliged to have answers ready in change situations, we tend now to "shut up" about them and give our teams a chance to suggest ways and means themselves.

If you can get your bosses to solicit your input on ways and means, that's a start. However, it does not always guarantee peaceful outcomes, as the next case attests.

Case 12. Caught in a Cross Fire

Presented by Teresa Siu, a specialist engineer in the oil industry.

We claim to empower people by allowing early team input into decisions. But I work for two senior engineers who argue over any approach suggested by the other. Sometimes these arguments get vicious. I try not to take sides, but tight deadlines sometimes force me to start working with one approach or the other, which causes the "winner" to gloat and the other to hatch sabotaging behaviors. I dare not go over their heads, but sometimes I fantasize about the bad old days when top management kept secrets, made up their minds, and ordered my two bosses to comply.

First Pass: Written Solutions From Seminar Colleagues

1. Convince them their positions are not so far apart.

2. When they clash, you might suggest they find a "subject matter expert" in the department, or an arbitrator at a consulting firm, and let that person's opinion be binding. You might save time and effort.

3. If you dare, wash your hands of this mess. Tell them you will start production only when you have a clear directive

from them or from the level above them. Meanwhile, go job hunting.

4. Perhaps you could diagram each boss's position as you see it. Then, present a workable solution that might allow production to proceed. Help turn their disputes into a disciplined and thorough team analysis from which many possible solutions—and even new products—could emerge. If you didn't see value in each position, I doubt you'd have hung around this long. Maybe today's rejected idea can be tomorrow's new development project.

Your Reaction: What Advice Would You Endorse or Add?

_____

_____

_____

_____

_____

Second Thoughts From Seminar Teams and Speaker

1. *Show how much they agree.* This will work only when positions are truly close; it will not necessarily break their habit of arguing. Worse, it makes you their tiebreaker, case-by-case. And, ironically, they may unify against you some day.

2. *A subject matter expert legislates.* Yes, you might be able to sell them on a technical expert or senior management tiebreaker, if there is a precedent for it at your company or at related firms.

3. *Refuse to start until they present you with a clear single directive.* Then go job hunting. The audience laughingly reversed the order on suggestion 3. Job-hunt successfully before refusing to work—or at least realize you are taking a risk with this approach.

4. *Create a process for analyzing and solving disputes, with helpful fallout for future products.* The audience was particularly enthused about this response. A subordinate engineer who would take the trouble to extract all the value from each position, surfacing every salvageable idea, would give the team a gift that keeps on giving. Next comes a tool that will help Teresa—and you—to exploit solution 4.

Tool Kit: Silent Graffiti—All-Hands Problem Solver

Let's get specific about this. Here's a problem-solving tool to help people create solutions, even from opposing ideas, for faster team action.
Good teamwork means deftly helping people to upgrade their own
solutions until all are satisfied. Imagine yourself in Teresa's scenario,
to illustrate. Instead of being upset that your two bosses argue so
hotly, you could choose to look at their heat as passion for the work
and strong commitment to a viewpoint. One of your options is to get
them to *stop talking* and *start seeing* more constructively. For that,
you could suggest a "silent graffiti" exercise. You could ask them to
join you in working silently on a wall chart.

- Boss A lists her solutions with all steps listed in order. (Or you
  could diagram it from material she proposed.)
- Boss B lists his preferred solutions alongside for comparison or
  contrast. (Or you could diagram it from material that manager
  proposed.)
- Now, all parties remain silent for the rest of the process.
- Working as a team, the three people connect any ideas that
  can be married or merged. You "X" any ideas that are directly
  opposed. You work during a brief timed session to connect or
  resolve everything you can.

When you reach an impasse, you are ready for a tiebreaker. It
might be you, or an appointed "subject matter expert." Conventional
wisdom says that you or the third party would now choose the best
route. But not so! All the third party needs to do is top off the chart
with any "overarching goal" or vital constraint that would help parties
A or B to unwind the deadlock. For example, they might be arguing
over using titanium versus aluminum. As a specialist, you might know
a reason why neither metal can be used. You might free them to think
of entirely different materials that would weigh little and wear well.
Then you would leave them alone again to reduce their disagreement
further. You prod them to find a third option.

Once they've done another round to reduce disagreement, you
might come back in to comment on their opposing ideas. Your comments might run like this:

> If I were to adopt your Step 5, Peter, my technical folks
> would incur this risk . . .
> If I were to adopt your Step 5, Martha, my team would
> incur this other risk. Could we continue proposing options
> until the risk is reduced or eliminated? As the performing
> team, we'll take any option that you propose as long as it
> looks workable.

In short, you'd directly avoid choosing the "best idea" and, instead, you would set up conditions that allow your bosses to find a third approach. You are proving your willingness to implement ideas that work—not to mediate a contest of wills.

Some people protest that managers don't have time for this sort of exercise—that a higher authority should simply legislate a way to go. But more experienced teams have convinced me that people on whom a brilliant solution is imposed can dampen it down until it barely works. Conversely, people helped to find their own solutions can enhance them until they work brilliantly. All-Hands Silent Graffiti is a good tool for gaining joint ownership of a process—a powerful motivator.

Raise Your Tolerance for Conflicts

In a multiple-demand setting, you must come to see conflict management as a natural exercise. A smart senior officer at a major hospital confirmed this at an on-site seminar:

> We talk openly about substantive conflicts: for example, hospital departments will normally conflict with chiefs of service; in companies, marketing groups will often conflict with production; it's natural for marketing to attempt to peddle things, available or not! Happens everywhere. Let people see that negotiating your way through these conflicts is central to the job, not some kind of peripheral hurdle that got there by accident and must be quietly removed.

A budget director for a state government office gave this advice in an interview:

> It's not always possible to get early participation rights for the whole team. But even if I cannot invite inputs on the "whether," I certainly solicit inputs on the "how" before things are locked down. While I don't feel obliged to explain and defend decisions made on high, I do explain, selectively, when I'm assigning work so that people can be at peace with the "why" of the assignment. I actively listen to doubts, and never fob anyone off with "Sorry, that's policy." If there's a split decision between me and a team member, I would rather invest effort in helping him upgrade his approach than in forcing him to take my view. I put in the time to get real accord because legislating flat-out seems fast at the start, but you pay in the end.

Using this officer's quote may help you win your point when bosses seem to cut you out of early participation in decisions.

An Illuminating Interview: The Blessings in Peacemaking

Here's a heartening story offered by the long-term executive assistant to the president, dean, and chancellor of a college in upstate New York. Her newly arrived boss, the chancellor, seemed to have a split personality—warm and engaging with pillars of the community, members of the board, and potential donors—but extremely chilly with so-called "common people," such as computer operators, maintenance and grounds people, secretaries, and administrative staffers. Even instructors got the remote treatment. This secretary got tired of hearing complaints and curious questions from people who wondered about this mystery man. She knew that remoteness would eventually erode this boss's ability to function. So she started a small campaign. First, she had little folders printed inexpensively, headed: *Congratulations from the Chancellor.* She would then scan the daily paper, looking for items about people around the college: their kids' sports achievements, cake sales, local stage performances, awards for bravery, and the like. She'd tuck these clippings in the folder with a note: *"Saw this in the paper. Thought you might like an extra copy for friends."* Signed . . . *The Chancellor.* These started going out. People started talking more warmly about the chancellor. Word reached high places that he was a caring and considerate man.

After a few months, she got more ambitious. She proposed to her boss that they start a little program called "Coffee with the Chancellor." Every couple of weeks, she would gather five or six people from various service departments. She would host the first few minutes of the gathering. The chancellor would come for the final ten minutes. (She'd have briefed him on the guests beforehand, so he could make small talk easily.) She assured the chancellor that this kind of event had worked wonderfully for other officers of the college in the past.

So the coffee mornings began. His involvement was easy and minimal, but the impact on his reputation was powerful. He soon began enjoying the results. She had fun, too, and was no longer seen as "The Ogre's Assistant." She added that the chancellor learned a thing or two about how interesting "the common people" could be. His newfound *noblesse oblige* echoed pleasantly in higher places. And her busy multi-boss life was no longer marred by negative comments and inquiries about her latest boss. *"I simply behaved like the good protocol officer every secretary is born to be,"* she chortled. Many at her seminar knew exactly what she meant.

Triumphs and Turnarounds: How to Redirect Your Energy

Another high-ranking government official reported at an on-site seminar:

> It's my main job to reassure people who are upset by shifting priorities or organizational changes. While others may hide out and isolate, we face sudden changes by joining forces in an informal exercise we call "circling the wagons." When a change or threat appears, we get together—the whole team. We use diagramming, humor, and performance measures to re-prioritize work and propose proactive moves. It's my job, too, to keep top levels off our team's back during changes until our team members have developed some strength and certainty. This reduces fear and infighting and keeps us alert to team concerns and needs.

Later, while he was out of the room, some of his direct reports commented that they'd gladly walk over hot coals for this man because what he said was true, and it had been demonstrated just a few weeks earlier during an RIF (Reduction in Force) that caused an agency-wide shake-up.

When you face complaints or threats about your plans or actions, ask:

> How can I focus on the future? What is possible now? How can I advance the action on this?

When you are asked to legislate between others in conflict, ask yourself:

> How can I help all parties to construct solutions themselves? How can I help them to preserve their processes for easier use in the next conflict?

Summary: Conflict Survival School

1. *Detach.* Give up practicing psychiatry without a license.
2. *You can't change people.* You'll pay if they catch you trying.
3. *Avoid disapproving of bosses.* It gains you nothing.
4. *Get clear about power conflicts.* These can be negotiated.
5. *Avoid taking on "people responsibility" with vague authority.* Either get the authority in writing, get it handed to you in the presence of the subordinate, or opt out of the deal.

6. *Settle peer disputes with peers.* All problems should be handled at the lowest feasible level and cost. Get boss approval to team solutions.

7. *Recruit subject matter experts to help settle disputes objectively.*

8. *Show subordinates how to process conflicts successfully if clashes exist or occur.*

9. *Accept conflict as natural.* Count resolution as a joint victory.

10. *In conflicts, focus on the future.* Empower combatants to make their own peace. They may invent a great third solution.

5 Stress Reduction Strategies

H ere's a vital fact to remember: not all stress is bad for you. Some of your stress can be exhilarating. Think of those weeks when your results amaze you, when your ingenious solutions thrill your bosses and customers alike! You may get tired, yes, but you go home feeling on top of the world. Those most challenging weeks of your life remain in your memory forever as peak experiences and proud achievements.

Now, by contrast, think of those weary weeks when you slog through endless heaps of trivia, when you backtrack over small errors made in haste, when you tack another patch onto a leaky system. You reap tinsel rewards; you feel thwarted and depressed. Stress doctors cite long-term frustration as the most dangerous stressor. It saps your energy and erodes your confidence subtly, remaining underground, unnoticed, and untreated, like hidden termite damage.

By contrast, you'll tend to react more strongly to large, imposed changes, especially when they hit with little warning or information. If your defenses go up too fast, your perception narrows. Embedded fears and biases blind you to the opportunities that may lie hidden in the change. Here's a case that illustrates:

Case 13. New Deal With a Catch

Presented by Oscar Gruschy, materials handling supervisor for an office supply warehouse.

Last month our boss announced we'll be restructured into self-managed teams. He handed out a folder giving details. We'll be doing more meetings about it, but mainly workers are supposed to do their own timekeeping, solve quality problems, assign their own work, and invent better procedures. Supervisors like me will do less bossing and more coaching. "What's the catch?" we wanted to know. Well, the catch arrived last week. Our boss brought in our new "coach"—a young girl of about twenty-five! She was hired over me and two other experienced supervisors who should have been up for promotion. Our old boss is still there, but she's interposed between us. She's supposed to be the expert on the new program, but when we bring her a storage or retrieval problem, she tells us to go think about it and propose our own answers. Not much chance we'll do that now.

First Pass: Written Solutions From Seminar Colleagues

1. *Give it time.* We've used self-directed teams at our company for six years. At first, it was hard for us to adjust, even with a background in teamwork and total quality. It took months of meetings and planning to make it work. If your company is serious about this, you are barely getting started. Don't worry, you'll get plenty of chance to comment.

2. *Change is stressful: don't make it worse with envy or suspicion.* Oppose this new supervisor for the wrong reasons (gender or age bias) and you could end up in trouble or in court.

3. *Your old boss is still around.* Get his advice on the new situation.

4. *Study up on self-managed teams.* There's a downside to everything, but we have self-managed teams in our company, and we're getting more say and better bonuses as team members than we used to as hotshot individuals.

Your Reaction: What Suggestions Would You Endorse or Add?

_____

_____

_____

_____

_____

Second Thoughts Expressed in Group Discussion

1. *Give it time.* New management structures don't gel instantly. Self-managed teams are not a "flavor of the month"—they are spreading because computers are making "virtual teamwork" practical. You'll do problem solving by e-mail or on your company's intranet with teammates from various specialties.

2. *Don't worsen stress by resisting.* Class members warned against "scapegoating" a newcomer when facing a

change. They guessed that the company's commitment to this new program was not triggered by this mid-level newcomer. She's an effect, not a cause.

3. *Get help from your old boss on how to adjust.* Don't complain to your old boss about the newcomer. Just ask his advice about *your* role in the new program, and ask about *your* next chance at promotion. The new system may turn out to enhance your chances.

4. *Study the folder your boss passed out.* Always focus on how to apply any new program that top management brings in. Get a reputation as a good applications guy. One class member advised:

> We started restructuring at our company to cure admitted problems in response time and quality. Just as in earlier programs, this rollout took months longer than we'd envisioned, but we've got quality up by 20 percent—and we've cut service delays by 15 percent. What is your warehouse trying to fix with the new program? Focus on that!

Consensus Recommendations

For smarter stress control, take your time reacting to major change. Give yourself permission to merely listen, take notes, pause, ask questions, pause again. Believe that you will have a voice and get a choice. Next, you might begin looking for items you can accept and items you can negotiate or restructure. Express confidence that your team can improve the bidding for the good of the organization. Work to stay open, calm, and detached.

New Choices in Stress Management

Bear in mind that dramatic structural changes like Oscar's are not the prime threat in working for multiple bosses. You are more likely to come to grief gradually from prolonged periods of unrelenting, minor stresses. According to Drs. Veninga and Spradley, authors of *The Work Stress Connection,* and Dr. Hans Selye, author of *Stress Without Distress,* you recover much better when you face major, dramatic problems than when you ricochet from one small foul-up to another. The toll is physical, not just emotional—here are the signs to watch for:

- When you're buried in trivia, do you feel bored even though you're working intensely?
- As pesky problems drag on, do you experience sleeplessness, crankiness, minor allergy flare-ups, rashes, more frequent common colds?
- Do you grind your teeth while sleeping, or continue teeth-clenching during the day? Does this give you facial pain and frequent headaches?
- Do you stare at the computer screen until you incur eye strain or neck and shoulder pain?
- Do you work longer and longer hours, only to find you make blind errors in the wee hours?
- Do you wake up tired most mornings?

These are the signs of physical stress from work frustrations. But the real danger is invisible: when one small stressor follows another without respite, your immune system keeps responding until it loses elasticity. Humans are designed to cope with large stressors occurring further apart; we need recovery time. Small nuisances piled one on top of the other can lay you open to longer-term health threats: hypertension, ulcers, diabetes, colitis, and the like. Because stress's effects are relentlessly physical, you need physical responses that are simple, consistent, undramatic, and discreet—remedies you can apply daily until you get lasting help.

Stress Saver Tools

Many stress and fitness experts recommend that you try some or all of the following physical measures. I like to add graphic tools to help you stay on target.

Keep a Physical Stress Diary

Pay attention to your body. Note those times of day when you get most irritable, or when work/life events make you uneasy or angry. (Most people stay in denial that they are feeling anything at all.) Note what you do to relieve those feelings. Do you take a quick walk, call a friend, take some exercise? Or do you grab some caffeine, nicotine, alcohol, or my favorite—chocolate? Do you give in to embarrassing bouts of temper? Can barely stifled mutterings be heard when people pass your cubicle? You can pick one type of stressor and your reaction to it—noting it daily on your calendar or personal planner.

Once you are aware of your physical responses to stress, you'll start choosing gentler responses to situations that upset you.

Try Four-Second Breathing

Recommended by many stress physicians, this deliberate breathing is practiced by many athletes. When a bad moment occurs, when you feel the urge to fight or flee, slow down for a moment. Now, consciously inhale—one gentle and deliberate intake, through your nose—to the full count of four seconds. This fills your lungs. Then exhale, through your slightly-parted lips, to the full count of four more seconds. This slow exhale is the hardest part of the process, requiring the most concentration. To help slow you down for your four-second exhale, try repeating some simple words silently in your mind . . . words such as: *"I . . . am . . . calm . . ." "I . . . am . . . c-a-a-a-l-m."* Let each word take a full second, with *"calm"* taking two or more seconds as you slowly exhale. Repeat this breathing pattern four times. It takes less than half a minute total. If you do it gently, no onlooker will even notice that you're doing it. Use it to center yourself during difficult calls or meetings.

The U.S. Olympic Biathlon Team uses this breathing technique to gear down from high speed to steady concentration during their winter event. You may recall the event: biathletes must first ski at top speed, then halt and aim and fire a weapon. They use four-second breathing to slow and steady both their heart rate and their trigger finger as they shift gears. When you repeat the four-second breathing exercise, you will slow down your heart rate and steady yourself. Controlled breathing is also used by pain clinics to help patients control chronic pain without drugs. Of course, people who practice meditation also combine controlled breathing with the chanting (silent or audible) of a soothing mantra.

Before using pain relievers or prescription drugs, try four-second breathing for its proven stress relieving effects. It works well for many people at times of physical or emotional exertion. The idea is: restore yourself, moment to moment. That equips you to take good care of the multiple requesters who seek your support, moment to moment.

Try Another Graphic Tool: Widening Your Window

Here's another tool with physical as well as emotional benefits. Call it "Widening Your Window." This exercise is designed to make you more relaxed, more detached, and therefore more resourceful during trying situations. When someone challenges or upsets you—in a meeting or on the phone—you use a window-widening technique to externalize the hurtful attack and minimize its impact. Suppose your team attends a large corporate meeting, and you are suddenly blamed for a missed requirement or deadline. Your boss takes up the challenge and holds forth on the subject. You are feeling indignant, but you are not on center stage. You take a sheet of paper and draw a tiny box in the center. That box represents the harsh judgment just made against your team. Now, you begin to widen the window around it. Draw a series of outer windows representing the varied strengths and capabilities you can use to extricate yourself or solve this problem. For an example of how it might look, see Figure 9.

As you widen your windows out further, you add thoughts like:

- I have three suggested solutions . . .
- We're smart, we're connected, we can get good data on this . . .
- Some lasting good can come from this dispute . . .
- This encounter will be forgotten by the end of this week . . .
- I'll be taking a vacation soon to recover from overwork . . .
- I have a life beyond this room . . .
- My loved ones won't care what I say next . . .
- This too shall pass . . .
- I have choices in this and all matters . . .

Your sketch begins like the sample in Figure 9. Soon, the unpleasant inner box (the incident) is surrounded by wider windows—those visual symbols that indicate your options are many. The venom of the original insult is contained.

Figure 9. Widening your window.

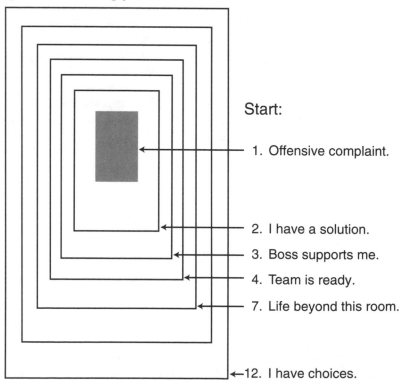

Start:

1. Offensive complaint.

2. I have a solution.
3. Boss supports me.
4. Team is ready.
7. Life beyond this room.

12. I have choices.

Many hospitals and stress control clinics use similar techniques to help coronary patients learn to calm and center themselves instead of flying into angry or anxious arousal when attacked. It is amazing to witness how steady and calm people can become when they practice using the window-widening sketch. Its personally comforting meanings help them to center their thoughts and regain physical composure. The upshot is: once you've drawn your windows a few times in privacy, you can toss off a new sketch without much concentration during your next heated encounter. All your attacker sees is a "doodle," but your widened windows take you "out there" past the momentary threat to your inner security.

Survey Responses on Helpful Applications

A few years ago, my company spent several satisfying weeks training and counseling a group of 150 senior and mid-level managers and supervisors from various departments of the state of New York in both Albany and New York City. These folks managed diverse areas like budget, education, mental health, social services, transportation—a whole gamut of responsibilities.

The course covered tools and suggestions like those just listed— tools to monitor attitudes toward work and stress, tools to control responses to stressful incidents, tools to eliminate self-defeating habits at work. These managers were notably dedicated to their work and supportive of one another's efforts to stay healthy. This is reflected in their comments in interviews conducted at critical stages of the continuing workshop:

- I did breathing exercises during the day and at the close of the day. Felt relief.
- Got out of the office for lunch three or four times in the last month. This makes me feel more energized for the rest of the workday.
- I found three things helpful: slower start mornings, "walk-around management," and brainstorming.
- Used shared calendar and wall lists for graphic delegation of tasks.
- Tried breathing and relaxation exercises to become more aware of some problems I was avoiding rather than tackling the work. I noted my specific reactions to stress on my calendar.
- I used a high-level alliance to get a problem stopped early.
- I am breaking the habit of doing "just one more thing before I leave." Decided at the close of the day to finish ONLY one item more, and ONLY if it takes fifteen minutes or less. End-of-day errors were negating any gains I'd made by staying on.

- Changed my travel pattern home: took small meditation "breathers" before hitting the traffic.
- I asked more *whats*—really putting the ball in the court of those who report to me. Delegated more assignments. I do follow-up only, checking less often than formerly. My old methods drove people crazy.
- I'm teaching more callers to speak to my staff—the people who know the detail on most situations. Long-term effect is a noticeable decrease in the number of daily calls to me, and more time to do essential decision making.
- I'm learning to say NO early. My old "anxiety-guilt" pattern is replaced by a new sense of "It's not all mine," and I am able to stay out of other people's interpersonal strife.
- I wrote a diary on "Why I am feeling pressured" and I saw that the pressure was coming from *avoidance* . . . so I got moving.
- I am seeing that the new respectful manner in which I delegate is bringing loyalty from my "troops."
- I delegated a whole project instead of just fragments: much more satisfying.
- I learned that some things can resolve themselves without my pushing.
- Changed my morning pattern: I get to work earlier for a reconnoiter before they all pounce.
- Started using a big red clip to reserve work for tomorrow rather than trying to stay and finish when I'm dizzy with fatigue. Found that my great secretary had knocked off some of it when she came in ahead of me the next day. I was able to thank her warmly. We both won.
- Used answering machine with "Tell me what you need" message. This has cut return calling time in half because I get back to people with answers.
- My spouse "kidnapped" me for a weekend at a local hotel after an exhausting round of meetings last week. I had talked with her about this course and my need to reduce stress. This was her novel way of helping.
- Showed a resistant subordinate—who usually wants *me* to decide before taking any risks—that there were *two options open.* Then I insisted: "You decide." I'm not over-hopeful yet, but I changed my half of the cycle.
- I'm learning to list my needs and speak out on the most important. Far better than *stewing!*
- I'm learning to act only when I can influence events. I'm doing the widened-window technique until I can see the true importance of an incident to my overall mission and career.

Survey Conclusions. You may note, as you consider the comments above, that these managers wrote diaries or made notes on their calendars. They gave themselves visual reminders and graphic progress checks to first increase awareness, and then make small behavior changes. Finally, their attitudes began to change, too. It all happened so gradually, they would not have been aware of the changes in themselves without their own written or graphic evidence.

If you begin writing a daily stress diary, your progress will reveal itself to you in ways you would otherwise miss. You'll get one more unsung benefit: you'll learn that your own approval is far more vital than praise from others.

Reduce Seasonal Stress: Ask Your Multiple Bosses to Help

The stronger you are, whether specialist or secretary, the more reluctant you'll be to ask for help with your stressful work situations. Some people will work uncomplainingly to the point of collapse, because they see anything less as weak or insubordinate. When questioned, some concede that they've been control freaks, unwilling to let go of a single detail no matter how much pressure they face. Here's a case in point:

Case 14. Month-End Crises

Presented by Parker Travis, an audit specialist.

Midweek and mid-month, I try to remind the management team of due dates without being a nag. But end-of-period crises pile up as our managers uncover last-minute changes that need senior management approval. Then, these "last-minute managers" hover over me as I rush to finalize their figures, with errors and tensions rising. Sometimes, we are forced to deliver late pages to audit meetings, one sheet at a time. On those nights, I go home totally drained.

First Pass: Written Solutions From Seminar Colleagues

1. *Chart people's required contributions in color bars on the wall or on computer.* If they are late, their bar stops short of its deadline. The effect on other dependencies becomes visible so that the boss and peers can come down hard on laggards.

2. *Submit figures to the big meeting with "holes" or rough estimates where the missing numbers were supposed to fit.* State right on the documents: "Numbers not available from

Group X." We do this with our boss's approval. Believe me, nothing more need be said—performance instantly improves.

3. *You may not be able to stop the last-minute changes that some managers make, but you can insist that requesters stop "hovering."* Just say: "I will have this for you by 4:00, and I will call you when the figures are ready. Standing over me will waste your time and make me nervous."

4. *Only when you diagnose the reasons for last-minute changes will you be able to stop or accept this practice.* What's going on? Are there legitimate new wrinkles that managers never faced before? Are there events beyond your company's control causing these last-minute changes? Maybe they are quite legitimate. I believe a lot of our stress incubates in the gap between necessity and our rigid ways of doing things. If you insist there is "only one way," it could be you who's out of step. Did management complain about that "sheet-by-sheet" delivery? Or were they actually grateful? Were you the only one who got worried and went home drained?

Your Reaction: What Advice Would You Endorse or Add?

_____

_____

_____

_____

_____

Second Thoughts Expressed in Group Discussion

1. *Performance chart.* Democratic because it tracks all contributions, a progress chart (paper or electronic) can help everyone hit targets. Visibility breeds peer pressure from all, not from just one team member like Parker.

2. *Expose holes in the report.* Often, the boss remains unaware of chronic lateness in a team because one member constantly sacrifices to hide others' sins. Yes, let the boss know about the source of delays; then let nature take its course.

3. *Put hovering off limits.* Ask for the quiet you need in a clear, courteous way.

4. *Check last-minute legitimacy.* Yes. Ask the laggard department what it would take for it to meet the deadlines that everyone else meets. You may learn of some special problem

in the department, and work together to correct it. Always ask questions about WHAT is still possible, rather than WHY something has failed in the past. Avoid the question WHY: it tends to elicit defensiveness.

Consensus Recommendations

By its nature, an audit will produce panic moments close to deadline. Vigilant teamwork can reduce but not eliminate surprises. Map progress continuously as you approach deadlines, or put crisis teams on problems early enough to stave off undue stress or error. Well before your next audit, put some routines in place to staff up and cross-train for the critical overloads that are bound to occur later.

Tool Kit: Recipes for Peak Workload Coverage

By the time you need crisis coverage, it's too late to start inventing it. Competent and consistent help must be bought and paid for in advance—if not with money, then with equitable barter arrangements. Here are some ways that deadline teams and overwhelmed secretaries are bartering for help in American companies.

Team-to-Team Coverage: Cluster Teams

Create a partnership with someone who can handle your level of detail, your level of confidentiality. Do it before peak loads hit. If your whole team gets swamped periodically, then expand to a team coverage. Secretaries at a major pharmaceutical lab created a solution they called "Secretarial Cluster Teams." Periodically, they faced huge documentation cycles required for the release of a new drug. The company had always authorized temporary typing help at these times, but the work required specialized vocabulary and more experience than "temp" services could provide. The secretaries lost too much time checking and correcting errors. As a remedy, they asked fellow secretaries from their other local plants to compare work schedules and begin trading off blocks of hours. One group would help another during special "swing" or night shifts—provided they could get an even payback when their own overloads hit. Intensive study, planning, and debugging took the secretaries three months. That year, the cluster teams saved the company $70,000 compared with previous coverage by outside contractors. This grassroots effort garnered a dramatic jump in both quality and on-time delivery. Morale skyrocketed when the company decided to distribute the savings back to the 100 secretaries who had hatched the new system on their own initiative! More important in the long run, management now saw the secretaries as a team of administrative professionals, cutting across all corporate functions. Their image changed from "clerical supporters" to "cost-savers" and "profit-makers."

Bartered or Budgeted Internal Help

Some companies allow internal groups to make formal contracts with each other for coverage. While no actual funds are exchanged, the deals are recorded to allow absolute equity in both work-sharing and gain-sharing or profit-sharing. In other companies, departments will bill each other for internal services rendered, using formal budget entries. Sometimes, helper teams receive bonuses or compensatory time in exchange for their services to internal groups. And in some commercial situations, we've seen teams of helpers spin off into subsidiaries of the parent, or into new independent contractor companies with strong links to the former parent.

Thaw That Hiring Freeze

Companies are serious about "no hire" rules after a reorganization. But they relent—if they must—to prevent performance defaults. Low-cost remedies include hiring students or retirees or recruiting volunteers who remain "on call" for peak periods. Instead of using "temp" agency helpers—costly per hour and expensive to train—these permanent on-call workers are trained once and reused as needed. Some companies guarantee on-call workers a modest minimum number of hours per week.

Creative solutions abound: In one Texas county with a hiring freeze, the call went out to retirees who could not afford to pay their county tax assessments. They were invited to work off the debt with skilled labor. They provided office help, accounting help, phone coverage, groundskeeping, cleaning—whatever their backgrounds allowed. Many of these people, after working off their debt, elected to stay and help out voluntarily. It's amazing what goodwill can be generated when non-profit entities use common sense. Your corporations might not seek free help, but you might use these ideas to recruit lower-cost help than you enjoy now.

Train Your Recruits More Easily: Use Index Cards

Of course, once you get help, there is no free lunch. You must train and equip your new recruits. And you can't wait until they arrive to start training. You make training investments early in the game to save time and waste later. Even before you seek permission to bring in help, you should be working on simple training tools. Write or sketch out an index card for each step of a process you will need to delegate. When you show your boss a "training pack" ready to use with a potential trainee, your seriousness comes through. Whomever you get, be it an internal barter colleague, a contract player, a student, or a retiree, you'll be ready to make that person effective quickly.

The big hurdle is admitting you cannot increase your workload indefinitely without getting help. Do not imagine that your die-hard efforts to go it alone will earn you admiration from on high, with attendant promotions and raises. Too many people have testified that when they left a job, burned out from the pressure, the company did not hesitate to hire two workers to replace them!

An Illuminating Interview: Thinking Beyond the Workload

Speaking of credibility and self-sacrifice . . . beware making assumptions about how much credit you can earn from good work performance alone. Most companies would prefer that you think beyond the workloads and ask for what you need. Here's a case in point:

When I met Marcia, she had put in more than twenty years of dedicated service at a family-owned business in Ohio. From the company's modest beginnings, she had worked as an assistant to the president and, later, to the personnel director. She had gained a lot of expertise in her role, learning much about business and personnel: recruitment, hiring, training, safety, development, performance reviews, wage and salary—the gamut. She had gained her expertise through experience rather than formal education, and she had not bothered to get a degree even though the company would have reimbursed her tuition. She was promoted to personnel manager under the director, she remained a confidant of the president, and she invested unstinting energy and dedication, handling increasing loads as the company grew from a few dozen employees to more than 1,500.

Though the personnel director was approaching retirement age, neither Marcia nor her bosses discussed future plans. Suddenly, at a routine physical, the personnel director was diagnosed with a health threat, and he took his doctor's advice to retire early. With many weeks of vacation owed him, he decided not to return to work at all. Marcia simply assumed that she would move up into the director's spot. As soon as she could clear the decks, she would ask to hire an assistant for herself.

She immediately went into high gear, taking on the work of her departing boss. Her lamp burned far into the night. The president tried to talk with her about planning for the future, but she asked for a delay, being busy with the now-doubled load. After a week or so, the president could delay no longer. He stopped by one evening, asking her to put her paperwork aside so they could talk. He started by thanking her for handling the transition so smoothly.

> "I'm giving you a bonus," he said, "and I want to assure you that this transitional burden won't last long. I've already interviewed a new personnel director and he will be taking over shortly."

Marcia was dumbstruck. She had been sure the job would be hers. She felt hurt, discounted, annihilated! Choking back tears of shock, she mumbled a meaningless response and fled from the office. Both she and the president made themselves scarce in the ensuing days, and Marcia did receive a handsome bonus check in the mail. The following Monday, the new personnel director arrived. His lengthy résumé had preceded him. He had worked for many small companies in the past, but his current work seemed to involve teaching at a nearby university, writing books, and doing corporate consulting. Marcia felt sure that her president had made a mistake. She decided that she could not allow herself to respond warmly to this new boss. She went on with her work in a dispirited fashion.

On the weekend, friends fanned her anger, encouraging her to quit this job. But privately, she feared putting a résumé together because of her mature years and her scant formal education. She began to feel betrayed and humiliated. How could she have imagined that the president saw her as a potential director, when all he saw was a low-level manager, barely past clerical worker? She discounted herself still more.

Worse, her new boss had scarcely arrived when he asked to sit down with her and "walk through" her workload. He put it this way:

> "I need to learn how you do things, Marcia—not to monitor or change anything, but to learn what you may need from me. I've been told you are carrying a very heavy load."

Marcia bristled at the thought of this intrusion. She resented having to "teach" him how to do personnel work. She doubted his abilities as a practical boss, and she showed him how she felt in many subtle ways. Late on Friday, her new boss asked if she would be willing to come in on Saturday so they could talk without the many interruptions that plagued them during the workweek. Once again, she felt put out, but she agreed. All Friday night, she tossed and turned, working up a head of steam that she yearned to vent on the new director.

When she arrived Saturday morning, he had coffee and pastry set up in the meeting room, and without further preliminaries he sprang this question on her:

"Marcia, what is it that you want?"

"YOUR JOB!" she flung back. "And I'm more qualified than you to do it!" She could hardly believe she was saying this. But the boss seemed unruffled.

"What *is* my job? . . . Do you know?" he asked quietly.

"I ought to know. I've been working personnel here for twenty years. Everything the personnel director did, I also did . . . but at a much lower rate of pay. Now, finally, when I should be given the director's slot and be compensated fairly for my work, I get a one-time bonus and a new boss instead."

"Ah," the new director returned. "But, you see, the work I've been hired for has never been done in this company. In case you didn't get to read this before, I want to point out something in the announcement of my arrival."

"I read it," Marcia snapped, her anger ditching her usual good manners. "You're an egghead."

"That may be," he chuckled. "But the real point is, I am an expert on taking family businesses public. That's right here in the announcement. That's what your president hired me to do, and that's why I am here: to help him steer the workers of this company through that process, and to avoid becoming unionized, if possible. We figure it will take only a year or two to get it done—and to launch the company on a new, much larger mission. Do you see?"

Marcia's eyes widened as she looked at the write-up clearly for the first time. "Oh . . ." she murmured. "I just didn't take that in. No, I didn't realize . . . I apologize."

Immediately she felt furious that the president had not bothered to tell her his real reason for hiring the new director. But she also admitted to herself, "That's not the new man's fault—and maybe I did make it hard for the president to talk to me."

"Marcia," he continued, "I've seen what you give to this company. You deserve a position much better than the one you have. The president wants advancement for you, too. I believe we can equip you for that while I'm here. Please use me as an ally, and let me help you get the promotion and the helpers you need, while I focus on my main mission, taking the company public."

In the weeks that followed, Marcia and her new boss planned carefully for her future. He credited her for all the aspects of personnel she handled so well. He also laid out the other parts of personnel work (legal issues, union/labor issues, and others) that had never entered her purview in the past, but that might do so now. Together, they worked out a program for formalizing her education and giving her the credentials to move up. He also began teaching her how to delegate. He convinced her that it was time for her to develop supervisory skills. She began to see that, in the newly constituted company, she would have a bigger, more rewarding job, but she still might not qualify as personnel director should the new man leave.

Soon, she joined the Personnel Management Association, and began meeting the high-powered people who held top positions around town. She learned, in a nonthreatening way, how much growing she still had to do. Above all, both the new personnel director and her president reassured Marcia that her job security had never been threatened, not even by her self-imposed entrapment in her workload. By widening her window, she was now readying herself for enhancements that would grow her job and her self-image for the next decade.

Triumphs and Turnarounds: Work–Life Management

Here's one of the more memorable lessons I've ever had about stress management. At an on-site seminar for a large liquor distiller-distributor, two mature women came into the classroom early, arm in arm. Their easy friendship and virtual telepathy were obvious. At a break, I asked if they were sisters—they seemed so alike.

"No," the younger of the two replied, patting her friend's arm. *"Ella's my work-buddy!"*

Ella broke in: *"Yes, I retired from the job that Lucy now holds. After a few months in retirement, I grew bored, so I offered to work 'on call' to cover peak loads and vacations."*

"Ah . . ." Lucy added, with a light in her eyes. *"That's how it started. But then, my husband was diagnosed with Alzheimer's disease. On many days of the year he doesn't know who I am, and he is looked after very well by a home care aide, so I come to work. But both the company and Ella have agreed that if I wake up any morning and find that my husband is himself—aware of who he is, and who I am—I can call Ella and she comes right in to cover the job. I can enjoy the rare day with my husband. That's so important to us. It makes Ella far more than a sister to me!"*

Ella added: *"I feel super-motivated on those days. I know I'm making a real difference in more places than one."*

Their company was well known in the area for sensitivity to family needs and work-life balance. Not only did the company offer help with child care and elder care financing, but they allowed employees to contribute unused sick days to co-workers in crisis. People at that seminar testified that no one abused the system. On the contrary, most people embraced the program with intense loyalty to the company and to each other. I've never forgotten the radiant faces of those two women, their joy at being empowered to do good. That power is the best stress-reliever in the world.

Schedule Your Work–Life Balance

Handling a multiproject workload can be all-consuming. That's why most good personal planner books and software programs include home and work sections on every page or screen. They remind you that life is what passes by while you're planning your future! There are many personal tools for achieving balance. Some people stick a simple note on the refrigerator or shaving mirror each day, with a pleasurable family or personal goal on it. It can be as simple as *put in a tomato plant, see that movie, call Grandma,* or *take a run after work.* Once they achieve these personal goals, they keep the notes in a stack as evidence that they are taking care of themselves. If too many notes remain undone, they put them into their day planner or check them against their computer schedule, knowing they must negotiate a cut or swap in the work schedule to accommodate life. Unless you write down or post personal goals, they remain invisible, and your frustration, though subliminal, nags away at you vaguely.

Some people use New Year's Day to write personal or family goals for the year. Often, the personal goal can be simple, inexpensive, yet fulfilling: joining the choir, learning to knit, gathering paint and fabric ideas for eventual redecorating, donating two hours per week to a charity or community effort, playing a new game with the kids, learning a language—whatever they want. Then they transfer these goals to their formal schedule. They write at the top of each week: *"What am I doing this week to pursue this personal goal?"* Because they schedule the pleasurable activity just as formally as a work obligation, they tend to do it.

Could you start using visual reminders, posted into your schedule in advance, to ensure spending more time on life? If you fail to remind yourself, you force your loved ones to nag. Their motives may be loving, but your response, given late, may be joyless. Give yourself a chance. Go visual with your life goals.

Summary: Ten Stress Reduction Strategies

1. *Reduce small hassles.* Welcome good stress!

2. *Openly inquire about imposed changes.* See how you might benefit before resistance sets in. You can always negotiate later.

3. *Try physical stress reduction tools,* such as the Stress Symptom Diary, Four-Second Breathing, or Widening Your Window when attacked or frustrated.

4. *Take a balanced view of stressful incidents.* Remember, you have a life beyond this job. Let no single work incident bring you down for very long.

5. *Flag your schedule to anticipate and cover peak seasonal traffic.*

6. *Pursue coverage options: barter, budget swap, thawing the hiring freeze.* Start using on-call part-timers or retirees for modest hours per week.

7. *Prepare training tools long before you need to delegate a task.*

8. *Enlarge your professional network and continue your formal education.* Don't let blind dedication block off your choices.

9. *Encourage your company to support work–life balance programs.*

10. *Make current life goals legitimate with visual reminders in your schedule.*

6 Assertive? Abolish the Thought!

L ook it up in a dictionary and you'll find *assertive* defined as: 1. *positive*, 2. *dogmatic*, 3. *arrogant*. Consider yourself warned!

Using definition 1, management gurus have made a big living teaching assertiveness to the fainthearted. On the other hand, strident practitioners of assertiveness have demonstrated meanings 2 and 3 far more often, causing prudent thinkers to look with suspicion on hard-sell assertiveness.

In the 1980s, books, articles, and courses on assertiveness were the rage. Titles such as *Games Mother Never Taught You* and *Winning By Intimidation* flew off bookstore shelves. To qualify as assertive, it seemed, one had to live in a constant state of alarm, agitating against insidious attacks on human rights. News reports abounded on abortion rights, gay rights, consumers' rights, prisoners' rights, the right to die, even the rights of small children to divorce their parents. Despite the complexity of the issues and the careful thought required to take a position, one's failure to stand up and be counted was condemned as apathy, cowardice, or surrender to some hated caste conspiracy.

Now the pendulum has swung very far from this notion. With a new millennium upon us, we see numerous press accounts mourning the loss of civility in American life. Companies offer seminars on etiquette for businesspeople who never learned basic manners at home or school. Citizens are cautious, even fearful, about asserting their rights with fellow motorists lest they trigger someone's "road rage." Supervisors hesitate to discipline workers; professors dare not critique master's degree candidates for fear someone will retaliate with a lawsuit or a handgun. In daily life, we struggle to balance assertiveness against basic self-preservation. At work we must neither wimp out nor war with our multiple demands: It's a minefield.

Nonassertion: The Price You Pay

If you stifle your own legitimate needs—if you say yes too often at work—you may be saddled with grungy tasks and unpaid overtime.

You may even find yourself blamed for other people's errors and omissions. If you comply with unreasonable demands, hoping you'll be thanked for self-sacrifice, you risk setting a precedent in which any feat short of a miracle will be dismissed. Physicians warn that allowing a steady stream of mild insults will exhaust your immune system. But if you face down a corporate villain, you're taking a risk, no matter how righteous your indignation. You could win the day, enhancing self-worth and prideful victory . . . or you could lose to an unprincipled manipulator with the power to take points off your next performance review.

Aggression: To Be Used Sparingly

Eventually, people too long victimized may explode into a sudden response that impacts them physically, like an unguarded sneeze. Both tormentor and victim are caught by surprise. The tormentor, accustomed to winning, may react directly with words that wither . . . or may retaliate slowly, suspending the victim in greater uncertainty than before.

At best, your surprised tormentor may back down, apologize, and appear to perceive, finally, that you do have boundaries. Having "erupted," you may feel better . . . briefly. But old behavior patterns easily return. The tormentor tests the new boundaries, and you start feeling guilty or fearful and begin to retreat. This puts your tormentor back in power. Now, you start paying the toll: You must try harder than ever to restore the familiar imbalance in the relationship. The tilt may grow perceptibly worse.

Explosions, even when justified and successful, seldom occur in a vacuum. You may get disapproving or pitying glances from onlookers, with comments like: *"It's too late now. You should have done this long ago."* This can leave you feeling more impotent and isolated than before.

Many smart seminar attendees admit to using an occasional outburst to wake up a "clueless" colleague or boss. If rationed carefully, these displays can sometimes get you the turnaround you need. Your reputation and work record must be creditable, however, and your self-esteem must be unshakable, if your sudden stand is to pay off.

Assertion: Recommended With Caution

Asserting yourself involves moderate risk with high potential rewards, but you must lead with courtesy and preserve your own dignity. Non-assertive behavior invites low-grade continuous abuse and erodes your self-worth. Aggression ignites sharp counterattacks from those who outrank you and those who can outgun you.

Do's and Don'ts: Assertion, Nonassertion, Aggression

If you want to spot what's going on during a tense exchange, look for these verbal signs:

1. Asserters say: *"I need . . ."* followed by a plain statement. Example: *"I need access to this data in order to finish this report."* Not: *"Could you do me a favor? Would it be okay if . . . ?"* For added courtesy, you might add, after stating your needs: *"Please tell me what **you** need. Our solutions should serve us both."* This kind of healthy assertion, done with courtesy, will often succeed.

2. Nonasserters start out: *"I may be wrong, but . . ."* or *"I'm only new here, but . . ."* While they may continue with a perfectly valid statement, they've already committed verbal suicide. Nonassertion never works.

3. Aggressors lead with the dangerous word YOU! They open sentences with: *"You should . . . You must . . . Why did you? . . . Why don't you?,"* then wonder what went wrong when others counterattack. Avoid the word in any tense communication, and never open sentences with that word.

Of the three choices, you could succeed best with the assertive: *"I need . . . tell me what you need"* formula. But there are options even better than assertion if you will take the time to consider and practice them.

Consider a New Pathway: The Five-A's Method

When you are frustrated or ill-treated, when you feel the need to assert yourself, but without undue surrender or aggression, you might consider the Five-A's Method, but you must consider it in advance, and practice it until it becomes routine.

ACCEPT . . . ASK . . . AFFIRM . . . ACT . . . ADVANCE

1. Accept. Accept what is. Understand whether you are in a position to lead or to follow, to demand or to serve. If you are hired to serve customers, if you are subordinated to bosses, accept that fact: perform that role at peak effectiveness. In short, be the best you can. Be the best trained, best qualified, most experienced, and most able server or specialist you can. That helps you to develop your center; your sense of mission and pride from which nothing can shake you.

2. Ask. Don't assume that others can read your mind. Often, you'll get all that you request. If you don't ask, you can't blame others for failing to notice your needs. You may earn new understanding and respect from people whose help you seek; often they are flattered at being asked. Ask for needed data, access, or new opportunities. Ask a person to change a behavior that causes you grief. Ask simply and directly for whatever it takes to facilitate an outstanding job. Show the benefits to others in meeting your requests for equipment, training, access, or help. Do your research. For example, be ready to show figures on the cost differential between working paid overtime and using a part-timer for those same hours per week.

3. Affirm. State, for your own and for your company's sake, your allegiance to your executives' goals. Show your bosses how you will add value to projects when you are included in the plans early. Learn and use the latest tools and upgrades in your area of specialty. Keep track of your proposals to save money and time. Give your boss a list of these contributions well before your performance reviews. Help your managers see you as essential to their work—as "one of us." Whenever your bosses are working on the biggest program or process of the month, you should be with them. Arrange it! When great things are happening, they should be able to see your face.

4. Act. Initiate more. Design and manage more projects. Don't wait to be asked. Volunteer to research and present proposals; show your managers how they will benefit by your early involvement in their plans and meetings. Get approval before taking major steps or spending major funds, but show that you can and will take initiatives. Remember, power is not given, it is taken.

5. Advance. Always move the action forward when talking, thinking, or responding. Whatever offense or error may have happened earlier, remember that you have maximum power *now* to make things right, to create new solutions, to improve situations, to make reparations, and to win new loyalty for your organization or team. Don't wallow in regrets, but build a new victory. Then, if you want to offer reparations for errors or omissions of the past, you are already in pursuit of recovery for your clients, your company, and yourself. Act from strength.

The Five A's: Practice Pays

Consider a multiple-demand situation in which you must choose an assertive response. Give the Five-A's formula some quiet consideration. You may discover that you've begun the process already. Pick it up at any appropriate point on the continuum: With Accepting . . .

Asking . . . Affirming . . . Acting . . . or Advancing, you can erase the negative image of assertiveness from the minds of your negotiating partners. Use the Five A's to reap greater respect, team harmony, and career credibility. At a series of seminars, we asked participants to consider some real-life cases and to apply the Five A's formula.

Case 15. The Client Godzilla

Proposed by Ulrich Kemp, an MIS project manager in a property development firm.

I have an internal client who considers himself superior to all other building clients. He irritates me no end when he says: *"I'm going to call you every day to make sure you keep my project on schedule."* He could out-assert Godzilla!

First Pass: Written Solutions From Seminar Colleagues

1. Accept. Accept that he is the customer. Though not "always right," each customer is always important. Let him call. Have your response ready.

2. Ask. Ask him which risks concern him so much that he is prepared to call you daily. Find a way to anticipate and cover those risks for him, so a daily call is not required.

3. Affirm. Affirm what you WILL do for him. Explain that not all projects make significant daily mileage, and show him the actual critical incident path for this type of project. Offer to call or leave word at those critical intervals. If you get him protected at vital points, he may get off your back.

4. Act. Improve his on-line access. Our customer service teams offer on-line check-in facilities so selected customers can be sure that milestones are being met. If you get him easy access to your site, he can study progress data for himself. This is one way we empower our customers.

5. Advance. If you do provide extra warnings for him this time, remind him that you are investing in building a process he can trust so you will not have to go the whole nine yards next time.

Your Reaction: What Advice Would You Endorse or Add?

Second Thoughts Expressed in Group Discussion

1. *Accept.* Some clients are more anxious than others. Accept that he needs more assurance than others, and find ways to provide that service at less emotional cost to you and an acceptable cost to your organization.

2. *Ask.* Can you arrange posting that data somewhere for him so he can readily see it? Can you fax him at set points? Are you networked on a LAN? Can you e-mail him on the Internet, at agreed intervals, reducing the need for him to interrupt you at random?

3. *Affirm.* Point out the relevant benchmarks in his project, those points at which most clients need reassurance. Give him access to progress data on those selected points only.

4. *Act.* If he misses a day, you call HIM. Resisting him will only make him more determined. Acting to assure him may quiet him.

5. *Advance.* Show him how much time and trouble you will invest now to build credibility with him later, because he is a potentially valuable customer. But if his business is not worth the trouble, *advance* him on to a new supplier!

Consensus Recommendations

The principle here matters most: As with any customer demand or compliance requirement, don't waste energy resisting, but get it done at the lowest possible cost.

The process can vary. Any of the methods suggested are acceptable; your ability to use them depends on your technical capabilities for communicating with customers. How cheaply—and how securely—can you automate the process?

Case 16. Negative Challenger

Presented by Vera Samposa, a bureau director in government.

Our multiple workloads have reduced time available for debate. How do I "turn around" an arrogant team member who fights newly announced policies or projects at every turn? With any new directive—about budgets, expenses, any compliance item—he unleashes a tirade of complaints and questions. He challenges me in front of the team, making me defend or explain each detail. Once he's satisfied, we can all proceed. With our workload expanding, I cannot continue to entertain his opposition.

First Pass: Written Solutions From Seminar Colleagues

1. Accept. Stay positive; assume that this person really needs more time to understand new projects. Whatever he asks you, you return the question to him: State that he must research and come to understand it by a deadline, rather than be spoon-fed by you. Meanwhile, say that you and the team must proceed because you already accept the policy, and time is pressing.

2. Ask. In private, ask him what he is willing to do to control his negative impulses and sign up with the team. Show him where his right to reasonable inquiry crosses a line into resistant behavior. Ask him to work on himself. Perhaps you can work out a signal to warn him when he crosses the line.

3. Affirm. Before you give this guy your rationale for supporting the new policy, affirm that all policies are compromises—that none need be perfect, only practical enough to cover prime needs.

4. Act. Whenever you present a new directive, invite the whole team—not just this one guy—to list anticipated questions they might need to answer for users. Then, have the team work out the clearest answers they can. This solidifies team commitment, and provides you with a tool for handling queries as the policy rolls out. It neutralizes this guy's solo power.

5. Advance. Make him aware that questions seen as helpful and well-meaning will get him approval. Warn that a pattern of constant quibbling could take "points off" at review time. He must produce, not tear down—advance the action, not delay the team—if he is to get ahead.

Your Reaction: What Advice Would You Endorse or Add?

_____

_____

_____

_____

_____

Second Thoughts Expressed in Group Discussion

1. *Accept.* Accept that every group has an official leader, using title and authority (like you) and also some unofficial "opinion leaders" (like him) who use brilliance, wit, or daring to engage the team. If your team accepts his long-winded challenges, they may see him as an unofficial leader. Some smart official managers would put his brilliance to use rather than fight it. But get him to exercise his brilliance "offstage," not during your meeting.

2. *Ask.* Ask the rest of the team to explain the new policy to him. Do this when you feel there is strong general support for the policy. Let team action take him down a peg.

3. *Affirm.* Affirm that you will entertain his comments only if they have been resarched thoroughly, to a level acceptable to top officials.

4. *Act.* If his arguments slow the team down, take him off the new projects and let the others get on without him. This may sideline him onto lower-level implementation of older, accepted programs. Let your "go-getters" work on breaking trail . . . make this "foot-dragger" work the repetitive details.

5. *Advance:* Warn him that no organization welcomes cheap shots when new programs are announced; instead, he'd do better to question new policies only if he can demonstrate a risk and offer a clearly better option.

Consensus Recommendations

Vera is this man's supervisor and coach. She needs to counsel him privately on acceptable levels of dissent. She must clarify that he will get credit for solutions, not for complaints. She needs to lay out consequences of his negative behavior and ask him to practice self-discipline in order to advance.

Case 17. Implied Promises

Presented by Walter Wilson, an aeronautics engineer.

After some strongly implied promises that I'd be next up for promotion, my main boss appointed someone else. I'm so disillusioned, I've clammed up for fear of what I'd say to him once I start in. I wonder if my other bosses know "why," but I'm embarrassed to inquire.

First Pass: Responses From Seminar Colleagues

1. *Accept.* For this assignment, the other person may be slightly better fitted. It's no reflection on you. Since the appointment is made, the matter is out of your hands . . . so try to let it go.

2. *Ask.* Ask *why* you were not appointed when you expected to be.

3. *Affirm.* Whenever a colleague gets promoted, even if you are upset, you would be smart to affirm to your boss that you will support this person without reservation. Your boss might be feeling guilty or worried about passing you over. This may or may not open him up, but it is likely to win you points for maturity.

4. *Act.* If you are too angry to trust yourself with the boss, find a reliable mentor (the best bet among your other bosses, or possibly someone outside your company). Ask them to be honest about any shortcomings *you* may exhibit; but avoid awkward questions about your main boss's intent.

5. *Advance.* Begin to create a "coming year" agenda with the boss, quite apart from this promotion business. What will the department need next in your area of specialty? What new projects will be needed? How can you get involved? Study the terrain and make the boss an offer. He may then reassure you of his overall plan and your place in it.

Your Reaction: What Advice Would You Endorse or Add?

_____

_____

_____

_____

_____

Second Thoughts Expressed in Group Discussion

1. *Accept.* This may not be about you at all. The big boss may have to pay off a debt or please someone higher. You're right to hide out until you can quiet your anger: Fighting now could hurt your future chances.

2. *Ask why.* This response elicited some loud "no's" from fellow participants. They correctly sensed that this might trigger your boss to defense or attack. They reframed the ques-

tion this way: Ask the boss **when** your promotion is likely, and **what** improvements or conditions would need to be met for you to be up for the next promotion. Ask **which** situations have changed since your last talk about moving up. If you are sure you were in the running for this promotion and lost, it's OK to ask the decision maker about any improvements you need to make to become more eligible. Don't ask *why* about their motives, ask *what* you should do next.

3. *Affirm.* Assure your boss that you believed him when he promised you a promotion and that you still believe him. Tell him your hopes for your next upward move—your plans for the things you want to do for the company and department—and ask for his advice.

4. *Act.* Whether you talk to a mentor or not, take some action on your own behalf, never against the new boss or his appointee. Use "being passed over" as a propeller: Do you need to take any technical or managerial courses? Is there some new technical area you should study anyway (even if promotion were not on the cards) just to enhance job security? If so, just do it. You'll be too busy to complain now—and you'll have a degree or qualification to show for it later.

5. *Advance.* If someone shuts a door on you, quickly open a window. Shop around inside your company, and get your résumé out to a few good places. Someone may make you an offer with which you can force your boss's hand . . . or an offer so good that your boss's promised promotion can't compete. While you're at it, show this résumé to your main boss: He may be looking right through you, failing to see how you've developed. You don't have to burn your bridges, but for myself, when I get bored or disappointed, I polish up my résumé.

Consensus Recommendations

Through thoughtful discussion, this seminar group endorsed the principle that "other people's behavior is rarely about you . . . but your choice of reaction is always about you!" The boss's decision to promote someone else may not have been about Walter at all. But Walter's pursuit of the question "What's next?" would benefit him for sure.

Several people liked the idea that you should present your boss with a current résumé whenever you are up for promotion. Don't trust it to memory.

Case 18. Idea Hijacked

Presented by Yolanda Abreu, production specialist, advertising.

I came up with a brilliant money-saving idea at a meeting. No one seemed to hear me. Within ten minutes, a department head—not my boss—repeated my idea and everyone jumped on the bandwagon. I was speechless. What am I? Invisible? Even when I shot a pointed look at my boss, he looked right past me.

First Pass: Written Solutions From Seminar Colleagues

1. *Accept.* Accept that this group may not be used to seeing a woman or a specialist in a leadership role. You will gradually change that. Until then, try out ideas first with your own boss; if anyone grabs your credit, let it be your own boss. At least he can reward you with good reviews and raises.

2. *Ask.* When you get a good idea, slip a note to your own boss and team first, so a lateral team cannot hijack you. With a stake in your idea, your boss or team could have supported you with: "Hey everybody: Yoli has a great idea there; let's open it up for discussion." But when you surprise everyone, even your friends may think you are grabbing the limelight.

3. *Affirm.* How about jumping up, thanking the "hijacker" for endorsing your idea, then taking It back?

4. *Act.* Sketch out a new idea on the flip chart so all can see it. That way, you keep ownership in the process. At worst, they might consider you just a note-taker, but you wouldn't be left in the dust.

5. *Advance.* Even if they do scoop your idea, you can still take an important role in working it out. You can say: "This idea actually started with my comment or question, and I want to be on any team that works with the idea. I have several more applications in mind." Volunteer to stay with it; then you might share in the glory.

Your Reaction: What Advice Would You Endorse or Add?

_____

_____

_____

Second Thoughts Expressed in Group Discussion

1. *Accept.* Accept that your boss may know better than you when the political climate is right. If the boss ignores your pointed looks at a meeting, move off center stage.

2. *Ask.* After the meeting, ask your boss to "educate you" on the interplay of people you just witnessed, and how to handle it next time. The unfolding events you watched may have had more to do with relationships and their history than with you and your idea. Your boss may start teaching you "Politics 101."

3. *Affirm.* A senior manager recounted this "affirming lesson" from her earlier days. *"What happened to Yolanda happened to me, too. When I complained later, a friend pointed out that I did not use conviction when I first spoke. I said something like: "I could be wrong, but . . ." I came across as uncertain. Others needed only that momentary lapse to grab my idea and run with it confidently. I can certainly affirm now."*

4. *Act.* Hijacking can occur, but much more often, your idea gets shot down in a meeting. If you still care about it, enter a reminder note in your calendar for each coming month. Keep reworking the idea until you've refined it into irresistible shape. Then retitle it, sell it to your boss and team, and let it come to life again.

5. *Advance.* Don't let this one incident turn you off inventing ideas. Just bring them to your boss first. Then, be prepared. He or she may decide to let another person present your idea . . . a person with greater clout or credibility. This may hurt at first. But you must ask yourself: *"Do I want the credit? Or do I want to see this idea fly?"* When you can willingly give up the credit, even pursue getting your idea "sold" by a more powerful person, then you know you have advanced in political savvy. You will find that bosses and people with clout will want you to be "one of them" when you have learned this lesson.

Consensus Recommendations

With political astuteness, course members agreed that you will often be tempted to present hot ideas spontaneously. If you do this, use strong, affirming language with no disclaimers. Don't be surprised if others try to run away with your ideas; it happens to everyone. If your idea is extreme—either fabulous or frightening—try it on your boss first; then seek the strongest presenter possible to float your idea.

Applying the Five-A's Method to Your Situation

How could the Five-A's Method help you win a boss, customer/client, or colleague over to your side? Choose a current concern, then pre-plan:

How I could use:

- Accept _____
- Ask _____
- Affirm _____
- Act _____
- Advance _____

to get greater advantage from this situation?

Supreme Assertion Test: Run a Meeting Full of Bosses

Earlier in this book, we covered meeting madness when you are the victim. Now, let's consider how you can win when you are the host or "perpetrator." You may have noticed that many audience suggestions have involved "getting your multiple bosses together" to agree on priorities, policies, and workloads. Well, here's another piece of practical advice: Run such meetings superbly or don't call them at all. A few essentials for chairing challenging meetings:

Agenda

- Keep it simple, short, and timed, so invitees know what time commitment they are making and what subjects they must prepare to debate or decide.
- Arrange items in order of impact, with high risk/value items first.

Meeting Process

- Provide "Living Minutes": List agreements on flip charts as the agenda rolls out.
- Allow no side issues to derail you: If people propose "red herrings," you can note these on a side board, not the main board,

and get back on track. Respectfully offer to discuss these side issues at a later point.

Participation

- Pre-test. In a contentious climate, don't go up against multiple bosses unless you've garnered support from one or two of them.
- Seek collaboration. When you sketch progress and agreements on a flip chart for "Living Minutes," take care to hand VIPs a marker so they can sketch their ideas and "own" the board too. That blesses it.

For the next meeting you plan—whether it's quick and informal, or a major negotiating challenge—think about using:

ACCEPT . . . ASK . . . AFFIRM . . . ACT . . . ADVANCE

as you plan both the contents and the process. If you do, you'll capture the number one meaning of *assertive:* positive! And you'll sidestep the dogmatic, arrogant tags with neat precision!

An Illuminating Interview: Assertiveness and Humor

Marty Franck is an administrative assistant for a large loan company. With nearly seventeen years' experience working for seven bosses at a time, she uses all the tools available: computerized calendars, project tracking, weekly team meetings. But it's still hard for her to stay in the loop and keep up with work overloads. *"My favorite secret weapon is my assertiveness,"* she confides. *"This skill took me a while to learn. It helps me overcome hesitation when I need clear instructions; it helps me limit the number and frequency of interruptions, and is always my first step in resolving conflicts. I don't hesitate to say: 'We seem to be working at cross purposes instead of together. What can I do to help change that?' "* She also uses humor, but warns that humor used inappropriately can shatter your credibility.

She believes humor works better when she makes sure *"the joke's on me,"* not on a boss or customer. *"I get them laughing and they become more flexible."* She works consciously to stay flexible herself. *"Priorities shift from hour to hour when you support seven bosses. Without flexibility I would be hard-pressed to put one task down, pick up and complete another, and then resume the first, all without turning a hair."*

Here are Marty's comments on the meetings she must often lead:

> I see meetings as opportunities to learn more about the company's business and to be seen as one who can handle

high-profile assignments. As a member of the Divisional Leadership Team, I'm called on to take on many assignments beyond the realm of typical administrative duties. Recently I served on a National Meeting Planning Committee. This group planned all aspects of our company's annual national meeting—an event attended by VPs, Senior VPs, Executive VPs, CFOs, COOs, and our CEO. I received this assignment not from my boss, but from his boss. I had an opportunity to prepare a project for him while my boss was on vacation, and he remembered my work.

Triumphs and Turnarounds: The Power of Affirmations

You've seen how affirmations can help you express goodwill and elicit positive reactions from opponents. But there are times when your opponent is you—when you need affirmations to convince yourself of the wisdom of a decision or action.

Of the nearly 200,000 people I've met at seminars, the most unforgettable was a public official, a man in his early forties, who approached me quietly during a seminar break to take issue with my statement that we always have choices. He spoke with intensity and a tinge of sadness.

> Pat, you might want to consider that some people have fewer choices than others.

After a moment he went on:

> I'm an example—I have a terminal illness. My life may end before I can finish the work that means so much to me. I'm doing a program for the disadvantaged youth of this state. I'm working as hard as I can, given my physical situation, but I know my health could crash at any time. So please realize that not everyone has a choice!

Though his situation was far more serious than I usually have in mind while teaching choices, I asked him to forgo the next hour of the seminar, to find himself a comfortable private corner in the hotel, and to write this affirmation: *"I have choices . . ."* until his anxiety eased. *"Nothing is so life-threatening as the conviction that you have no choice,"* I repeated. Once again, I asked him to settle down and fill a sheet of paper with the "I have choices" affirmation. *"Keep writing it over and over until new choices start occurring to you,"* I urged him.

"Are you sending me off to write five hundred lines on the blackboard . . . like . . . I am a bad boy?" he inquired, with his sense of

humor still operating. *"No,"* I answered. *"The writing is designed to help you focus, to blot out all other thoughts except one: the conviction that you really do have choices."* I told him that it mattered far more for him than for most people to see that he would continue making choices until he drew his last breath. He went off. After lunch, he turned up to tell me:

> Hey, it's working. I began to see choices about those parts of my work I could delegate, and therefore, those pieces I must focus on for the time I have left. Unfortunately, on those parts there's no one who can help me.

"Oops, there you go again," I prodded. *"Now, you'll have to go back and write:* **"There is someone who can help me."** He laughed and went off dutifully once again.

At the end of the day, as I was packing up to leave, he returned. I was amazed to see the change in him. He was jubilant.

> I wanted to let you know before you go. I wrote those lines for quite a while, and I thought of just the person to help. He's retired from this kind of work . . . he's nearly eighty years old. I'm ashamed to say I have not spoken with him for five years. I hardly dared call him. But to my amazement, he's still active and a lot more healthy than I am. When I leveled with him about my predicament, he offered to begin immediately on a *voluntary, unpaid* basis, working full time if I need him.

His eyes were brimming over as he went on:

> This wonderful man is dedicated to exactly the same outcomes I am seeking. In fact, he dropped what he was doing today, and he will join me here shortly for dinner to talk things over. I can hardly believe it. I can't tell you how grateful I am [*he said, taking my hand*] because for the first time in months, I feel hope!

Seeing that man's face as he spoke, realizing the hope he had reawakened by concentrating on what was possible—that was worth a thousand days of ordinary seminars to me. Whatever the outcome of that night's dinner, a miracle had already occurred: One person was willing to come out of retirement to make a difference, and another was prepared to use his last ounce of courage and strength to complete a mission. It took a few exercises in affirmation to help him find new choices.

I could barely speak as I gave him a goodbye hug and ran for the airport van.

Summary: Find Your Right Level of Assertion

1. *Try the assertive formula. "I need . . . tell me what you need."*

2. *Avoid disclaimers. "I could be wrong, but . . ."* Avoid aggression: don't open sentences with *you.* Avoid asking *why* about another's motives.

3. *Consider the Five-A's Method: Accept . . . Ask . . . Affirm . . . Act . . . Advance.*

4. *With customers, set boundaries, but give them access to data that will reduce their anxiety.*

5. *If subordinates tend to buck policy, have them write a thorough defense of the policy.* Set up team discussions so workers can defend new policies with clients.

6. *Affirm that you will support people promoted above you, especially if you feel "passed over"; then negotiate for the next round of promotions.*

7. *If you have a radical idea, try it on your boss/team first; don't demand support if you choose to "spring it" in an open meeting.*

8. *Note rejected ideas on your calendar.* Keep refining them until they sing!

9. *When things look bleakest, affirm that* **you have choices.**

10. *When you feel depleted, affirm that* ***someone can help you!*** *Then* ***ask!***

7 The Delicate Art of Delegating

As you accept more and more delegated tasks from multiple bosses, you reach the day when you, too, must delegate. Your multiple bosses may want you to maintain sole charge of all your tasks, but you may have to convince them they are safe, with you accountable for your delegates' performance levels. You—and they—may fear spending the modest amounts of time and money that delegation requires. But these are not the main barriers to delegating. The biggest roadblock is pride.

If you find yourself hesitating, you've not alone. It's hard to give up familiar tasks that earned you praise and recognition—especially if you are giving them up to tackle new, unexplored, and riskier matters from your multiple bosses.

Need Some Excuses?

You can always delay your D-Day (Delegating Day) for a time. You'll have plenty of co-conspirators, too: complacent managers and envious co-workers. In fact, co-workers who would never think to ask for a part-time helper will blithely borrow your new helpers for their projects, if you let them. Perhaps you've found it easier to hesitate, resting on one of the classic excuses for putting off D-Day:

- There's no one available; we're in a hiring freeze.
- It's quicker to do it myself.
- No one else will do it as well as I.
- The work is highly complex or confidential.
- If the helper botches the work, I'll have to fix it.
- I'll lose direct touch with some of my bosses.
- An ambitious delegate might try to outshine me.

Or you could simply face facts and admit:

- Delegating means hard labor: I must recruit, teach, critique, re-train, and supervise someone.
- I must plan work far more carefully if I am to delegate it.
- At first, it will be time-consuming; it's quicker to do it myself.

You're right. It is quicker to do a task yourself—**once.** But if you choose the right tasks—things you normally do daily or weekly—you'll amortize your training investment handsomely once the learner performs the task fifty times per year.

How You Know That Your D-Day Has Arrived

- You're working more overtime, more often.
- You lug work home when you're too tired to stay at the office.
- You miss important meetings or rewarding trips because you are bogged down at the desk.
- You depart for vacations, frazzled, and you keep phoning in.
- You hear yourself complaining: *I've got so much work to do for my managers, I can't get my own work done!"*

Your managers are right to delegate work to you. By the same token, you may be right to push work down to the lowest level where it can be done reliably. Now the question is, which work?

Find the Tasks to Delegate

The same pride, perfectionism, and drive that make you a great manager, secretary, sales pro, or technologist can get in your way when D-Day arrives. If you design, test, and perfect a procedure, you get emotionally attached to it, clinging to the labor long after you have maxed out the value. Scrutinize your repetitive routines—functions like order processing, data inputting, invoice preparation, travel booking, factual research, and expense reporting. For most of these, you have built SOPs, standard operating procedures, that work reliably time after time. In fact, face it: Your routines may work so reliably that users and requesters take them, and you, for granted. If you don't bother to value high-risk work over everyday routines, why should anyone reward you for it?

Start discriminating now. Even among your regular routines, there are major differences in risk and value. Start listing your daily or weekly jobs on paper.

Make two columns, as shown in Figure 10. Retain more tasks from the first group, delegate more tasks from the second. Put tasks to this further test:

Figure 10. Finding the items to delegate.

TASKS High Value, High Risk, or Hard to Manage	ROUTINES Well-Formatted, Stable, Easier to Manage
Project recommendations	*Daily summary*
Write/edit new report	*Final typing, any report*
Negotiate new site	*Renew with established site*
Create new performance code	*Monitor weekly compliance*
Create new file system	*Clean last year's files*
Purchase new equipment	*Monitor maintenance*
Interview complaining customers	*Research customer files*

- Can we eliminate the task altogether? No?
- Can we postpone and retrieve it later when we're less pressed? No?
- Then, we have to get help. Who?

Look for Help in Unusual Places

Find a person, less experienced (and less expensive per hour), who can follow where you led. *"What person?"* you may well ask. With budget cuts, hiring freezes, and downsizing, your managers may seem deaf to your pleas for lower-level help. You must search among low-cost options:

- Look for volunteers. Particularly in non-profits and public service organizations, you will have great success recruiting volunteers if you offer short hours and flexible schedules, and if you emphasize the value of the mission. Accept modest hours at first. Successful delegators say: *"If you can get a regular, repeat, reliable helper for as little as two hours per week, go for it!"*

- Look for help among recent retirees from your own business who can perform valuable work—especially contact work. They'll be sensitive to your customers' needs, and they'll require very little break-in time.
- Recruit college students. Many are technically trained to do drafting, designing, writing, proofreading, many computer functions, and other skilled jobs for a combination of class credit and modest pay. Bear in mind that research is the primary work of college and graduate school students. Let them hit the library or surf the Net while you do work requiring mostly discernment and decisions. It's moral: Remember, esteemed author James Michener often used large staffs of researchers when preparing his mammoth sagas. Would we have insisted he do them unaided?
- Don't shun high school apprentices. Many companies use these youngsters for inputting, bookkeeping, record-keeping, assembly, copying, shipping, and other repeat functions. The students welcome practical experience for course credit at modest pay.
- Finally, swap some time with fellow employees whose peaks and valleys contrast with yours. With confidentiality covered, you can bank on regular relief from in-house sources. It takes some effort to find and cross-train your "cover partners." You must observe fairness scrupulously, but the payoff is unquestioned.

If you still feel reluctant, do some simple math. Think of a task you handle now, a task taking as little as four hours per week. That adds up to two hundred hours per year, at your current rate of pay. If you can assign that work to someone who earns only seven or eight dollars per hour (or less), calculate what you'll save the company in a year, compared with your more costly hours. Then use the hours saved for higher-return work. If you are paid for overtime, the savings will look even more dramatic.

Break some of your tasks down into parts: Distinguish those pieces involving judgment from those elements that are mechanical or repetitive. You'll remain accountable for the final product, but delegate some of the details. Yes, you'll have to train, inspect, and bear the responsibility for quality. But you will not need to take every step yourself. And you will build depth and risk coverage into your team.

Cut Through the Boss's Confidentiality Barrier

Some of your bosses will be very sensitive about who sees or does their work. Perhaps you've watched personnel or accounting professionals stagnate in their careers because they get mired in confidential details. If you fail to categorize data by different levels of secrecy or risk, you're stuck managing all of it. Delegate the cooler items; reassure bosses that you will handle or protect the hotter ones. For example, at one drug-abuse clinic, staffers fell behind in transcribing and managing clinical notes. They needed to bring in help, but the privacy of patients had to be protected. So they assigned a code number to each patient. Once corresponding identities were kept under lock and key, volunteers could input and index data on treatment plans without violating patients' privacy. Has a boss trapped you in some task because of confidentiality?

No Age Limit on Trust

One of your bosses may cite experience or longevity as a bar to your delegating work. But there are safe precedents: One small manufacturer uses a high school student to run its weekly payroll. This youngster is accurate and conscientious. Furthermore, she ignores "payroll politics" because she is not competing for promotions or raises with full-timers on the payroll. This youthful outsider can handle confidential work more calmly than many a long-timer with an axe to grind.

While you work to shed your role as "keeper of the keys," you will need to shield your delegate from communication blunders. Make one blanket rule about answering prying questions: Your delegate sends all inquirers to you. That way, the newcomer need not pick and choose which questions to answer—for therein lies the trap when manipulative "elders" snoop around inexperienced helpers. Your delegate can be taught to say: *"I'm on a deadline, so my boss wants all questions referred to her."*

Delegating is difficult, especially to inexperienced helpers. Don't let a bumpy start deflect you or your bosses from the legitimate need to delegate. Here's a case in point.

Case 19. Too Hasty Help

Presented by Zack Maffeo, a manufacturing scheduler.

I'm swamped by multitasking, so I asked for help. I should have checked the list of available people first. They gave me a know-it-all who never listens, barges into tasks, and gets them wrong. He races to the finish, then we drag ourselves slowly through corrections. My time problems are even worse than before, and my bosses are regretting they ever let me bring in "help"!

First Pass: Written Solutions From Seminar Colleagues

1. Try releasing work on a gradient of difficulty. Release easy and repetitive tasks first. Leave difficult, decision-type work until later.

2. This sounds like a training problem. Break the task down into smaller units. Be sure he has one unit clear before moving to the next. If he has to keep repeating a unit until he gets it right, he'll get it right.

3. Have him check in with you before moving past the more risky or difficult steps. If he simply races through things, tell him how much time to allot to doing various steps. Show him that he must slow down and check with you at agreed milestones so he can't go too far wrong.

4. Who said that delegating would be timesaving? It takes more time at first! You invest time now to save time later. Take half the blame for rushing, but warn him how long he has to make good or fail.

5. Thank your bosses for letting you get help. Remind them that you'll train him just the way they trained you, given time.

Your Reaction: What Advice Would You Endorse or Add?

_____

_____

_____

_____

_____

Second Thoughts Expressed in Group Discussion

1. *Release work on gradient.* This means writing or sketching out the whole job and showing the learner which parts he must master first. Few delegators are willing to do these vital steps. Too many jobs are transferred quickly and verbally. The written or graphic approach takes time but reduces failures.

2. *Teach a unit at a time: require repetition.* Same as above: Requires written or sketched-out instruction for a job. Slap-dash here means grief later.

3. *Set time estimates on learning segments: regular checkpoints for safety.* Seems like a pain in the neck, but manufacturing standards demand it.

4. *Take half the blame for rushing; warn about "time's up" schedule.* If you've been doing a task for a long time, your movements may be fast and automatic. Others, watching you, will try to match your speed even though they've developed no facility. It's easy to forget how long you took to learn steps that have become second nature for you. Often, too, you teach steps as if they all deserved the same attention when, in fact, two steps out of every ten are the really critical steps. If you don't know this clearly enough to teach it, how can you expect a learner to differentiate? Set clear standards, retrain, reevaluate. If the person doesn't make it, replace him while he is still on probation with you.

5. *Right.* If you sense boss impatience with your delegation efforts, reassure them of your corrective program. Even if this trainee must be replaced, remind them you still will need help. Don't let these managers feel unrewarded for saying yes to your request for help.

Consensus Recommendations

Winning the right to delegate is so tough that you must doggedly motivate your bosses and yourself through the long process of planning, protecting quality and confidentiality, and building performance strength in your learner, no matter how much patience it takes. Don't waver in your determination to make your first delegation effort succeed; don't let your bosses lose faith. It will be very hard to lift this torch again once you put it down.

Delegation: Rewarding and Difficult

To gain the attractive rewards of good delegation, you might want to consider and follow ten steps that make this challenging process succeed better than it did for Zack in Case 19.

Steps One Through Ten of Good Delegation

1. Write up the task clearly.
2. Build in checkpoints for control.
3. Select the right person.
4. Make the task attractive.
5. Teach the job, face-to-face, step-by-step.
6. Allow two-way, open feedback.
7. Revise and reset goals.

8. Set up a self-monitoring plan, but don't stifle performance.
9. Provide operating support.
10. Reward effort.

Here are some clarifying details:

Step 1. Write Up the Task Clearly—Long before you recruit help, you can be writing up quick index cards listing the steps in some of your routines. Show your "card pack" to your bosses to convince them you will be ready to delegate when they say the word. If you wait until you are desperate to delegate, you will be tempted to skip this step or do it in haste. Failure at Step 1 does the most harm to the ultimate performance.

You may think that writing up a job is too much trouble, that any intelligent person will get the point simply by watching you. But prove it to yourself. Take some simple mechanical job like "stuffing brochures into envelopes." (Not the kind of task we do by hand anymore, but it is generic enough to be understood by all of us.) Imagine sitting down to try this task yourself. What questions would arise immediately?

1. Where do you put the stack of brochures? Right or left? Which side up?
2. Where do you stack the envelopes? Right or left? Which side up?
3. Do you open all the flaps before you start, or do them one at a time?
4. Which hand do you use for which motion?

Note what you would actually do, movement by movement. You'll be amazed at how many options there are—many of them clumsy—to get this job done. Now, imagine doing the same careful instruction on a task you must delegate soon. You have a recruit, let's call her Barrie, who is eager to take on the job. Don't be tempted. Before even approaching her, try the job yourself. Watch yourself. Jot down the steps, one per card. Rearrange the cards and confirm the shortest and best steps. Put the cards in final order. Simplify your wording. Use short sentences, no paragraphs; stick with a list of bullets.

Happy with your list? Think you're done? Try having a ten-year-old read it aloud. Watch the places where the kid stumbles or expresses doubts. Rewrite. Try the new version on another innocent reader. Once you are happy with your list of "do's," decide if you must add a shorter list of "don'ts."

Writing job instructions is one of the toughest but most rewarding aspects of delegating. When you hand those cards over, Barrie can take possession, make her own notes, play the task back for you, and demonstrate it. When she makes her final corrections on those cards, you know that Barrie's got it! You know early.

Step 2. Build in Checkpoints for Control—Any job you delegate will need controls on quantity, quality, budget, materials, and the like. State these limits clearly in your instructions. For our example, if you want Barrie to stop, to seal and bundle those envelopes in fifties or hundreds as she goes along (so you can get them into the mail in batches), you'd need to say so. Otherwise, she may stuff all 10,000 envelopes before sealing any.

If there are pitfalls, questions, or checkpoints to be observed, say so and highlight the correct intervals. Again, show these details to your reluctant bosses before asking for help; convince them that you will remain accountable for outcomes.

Step 3. Select the Right Person—Choose a person with the skills you need: algebra, drawing, specific software, layout and design, Internet skills, speed, agility, strength, and so on. Match the job with the person. But look for willingness, too, which can cover many learning gaps. Find a person who'll care about doing it. One of your surprises in delegating "drudgeries" is the delight a neophyte may take in doing them. A learner may need this new experience for his résumé much more than you need a reiteration in yours.

A word of warning: If your boss agrees to let you delegate, ask the boss to stand well back from the process. In too many instances, your boss chooses your helper and establishes a direct reporting line with the helper, and leaves only the day-to-day training and grooming to you. The trainee fails to "bond" with you—and feels free to override you. Don't allow this ambiguity; it kills your chances of success. It is so common, you really must move energetically to prevent it.

Step 4. Make the Task Attractive—Enthusiasm for work does not transfer automatically. You'll have to make a concerted effort to attract your appointee to the task. Appealing to the person's competence, you might cite specifics:

> Pru, most people work here six months before we let them try these calculations, but you were so quick and accurate on the ledgers, you seem ready now. How do you feel about it?

Or you may want to challenge a helper:

> Jake, we've got a discipline problem on the production line. With your counseling background, you may get a better reading on what's going on than I've been able to get.

Jake may relish solving this puzzle. Or you might ask a favor—swapping a task you don't enjoy anymore for someone else's routine, which has become tiresome for them. Thus, two more people are cross-trained on two sets of tasks.

Admit that others may succeed where you failed. Don't hesitate to delegate a communication task that has become unpleasant. If you've developed friction with a regular contact, there is no harm in delegating this contact to someone on your team who feels perfectly at peace about it. You are not always the best or only person to deal with every contact.

In all cases, couch your delegation offer as an attractive opportunity, not a desperate plea. A person who says:

> I'm swamped, Casey . . . can you help me out, please . . .

may scare away a delegate. You might do better by saying:

> I'm swamped, Casey: I need your help, and I'll make sure the boss knows that you are making a difference in this crisis.

If the job has intrinsic appeal or credit attached to it, say so right up front:

> Shirley, there's a chance for you to take over our monthly sales report. That means sitting in on the client meetings in San Francisco. You've said that you want to travel a little, and you've already shown the skills to discern and summarize meeting results. This role will get you noticed and possibly promoted. It did that for me. If you feel like trying it, I'll check out your first report with you before you submit it; I will also be available by phone if you hit any snags during your first meetings. What do you think?

Step 5. Teach the Task, Face-to-Face, Step-by-Step—In their haste to dump a task, many people begin delegation at Step 5, not Step 1. This practically guarantees failure. Keep this step where it belongs—*after* the trainee's interest is aroused and your written job instruction cards have transferred ownership.

Now, set up a quiet, uninterrupted session, at the learner's convenience, if possible. Let the trainee read through your cards. Invite any immediate observations:

> Any questions right off, Barrie? Which steps look familiar to you? Which ones look less familiar?

These are "open questions." They begin with words like: *which, when, what, where,* and *how:* These words will prompt a sentence in reply. Avoid closed questions to which a person can reply yes or no. Avoid asking: *"Do you understand?"* The learner feels almost obligated to say yes.

Instead, ask: *"What did I leave out?" "What should we run through again?"* This process leads to a dialogue, always more valuable than a monologue. Now demonstrate the job, step by step. Then, let the trainee try it.

Step 6. Allow Two-Way Open Feedback—Let the trainee complete the recital. Save corrections until the end. Let the person run through the process uninterrupted (unless she interrupts, herself, to ask questions). Just give nods of encouragement and "Uh-huhs" to let them know you are tracking with them.

When the trainee is done, you will then be able to say:

> Barrie: that's great. You got eight steps right out of ten. I'm not sure I heard you right on Steps 4 and 6, so let's revisit those two.

This puts Barrie at ease. She's got it 80 percent right. She feels competent, not criticized. (Had you stopped her at Step 4, she might have clammed up at the remaining steps.) Patience silence really pays off here, for the uninterrupted trainee will often revisit and correct herself as the steps continue to unfold.

Inviting open feedback takes practice. Avoid saying things like:

> I'm confident you can do this, Barrie.

It will be hard for her to argue. Instead, say things like:

> How do you size up the job, Barrie? Most people have some questions, some misgivings. Which aspects puzzle you?

Wait for an answer. Don't ask:

> Do you think we allowed enough time?

Ask:

> What do you think about the time span allowed?

Open your questions with:

- *What do you think about . . . ?*
- *What ideas do you have about . . . ?*

- *How do you feel about . . . ?*
- *What would you like to see done about . . . ?*

Step 7. Revise and Reset Goals—It may turn out that Barrie has a different idea about some part of the process. If her way is truly simpler, then adopt it. There is nothing more encouraging. On the other hand, you may see some risks in her revisions and have to reject them. Suggest that you may need time to think it over, consult others, and therefore delay approving her new ideas. Be forthright about the potential risks you see in the suggested change. Otherwise, the trainee may feel rejected personally. Often, a trainee will then stifle further suggestions but still make the changes, unilaterally, once on the job. That's bad for you.

Now work together to set both learning goals and takeover goals on this job.

- How quickly can Barrie expect to learn the inventory codes?
- Should she expect to do fifty entries per hour (as you do), or should her learning goal be more conservative to avoid errors? You may both have suggestions about this.

Agree and test in safety. As you agree on goals for speed, accuracy, wastage, and so forth, write them down. This set of notations will constitute your eventual contract or commitment. Be sure to include standards for:

- Quantity: how much, how soon?
- Quality: what room for errors, omissions, estimates, revisions?
- Costs: any limits on space, supplies, time, help?
- Latitude, access: any limits on who the trainee may consult, what approvals are required for release of work, how to handle inquiries?

Step 8. Set Up a Self-Monitoring Plan, but Don't Stifle Performance—Most delegators reach Step 8 in a hurry to wrap it up. Be patient. This is no time to abandon your trainee. Decide specifically how much supervision this delegate will need. Delegates differ: the neophytes may want you to stick around. "Experts" may want you to step back. Spell out, jointly, what the controls should be. Decide if Barrie wants to check in with you once a morning, once a day, or after a specific milestone. Will she check by e-mail, phone, or in person? Who will stop by to see whom? Will you want exception reporting only, that is, she contacts you only if a problem arises? The person's level of experience and maturity should dictate. If you fail to specify, the trainee will be forced to hover around you, wringing her hands—or she'll be forced to wing it when she really does need help.

Step 9. Provide Operating Support—Most delegators omit this step. When you delegate work, you must inform interested parties that someone new is now doing what you used to do. If your trainee expects information and cooperation from others, you must inform these others that you expect them to give Barrie the same excellent cooperation they have always given to you.

As you've learned in your own career, there is nothing more arduous than trying to do a job when no one knows you are authorized. Indeed, unless you authorize your trainee, some managers will think she is sticking her nose in where it's not welcome. Support the person you delegate. Once you've informed a department head that Barrie is now doing this work, you may still have to provide further reinforcement in writing. Give Barrie a memo she can wave when people fail to follow through for her.

Step 10. Reward Effort—First, two principles:

1. Good work deserves recognition. Make your thanks public.
2. Mistakes require correction. Make corrections private.

If Barrie does a great job, tell her so. Tell her when the boss and others are around. Your boss's delight will reflect on both you and Barrie. Be prepared, however. Despite all your careful groundwork, not all assignments succeed. After sincere efforts to retrain, it is kindest to admit early if someone simply does not show the skill level required. Some people lack the eye for layout or the mind for math that a task demands. If you see that a handover does not proceed well, don't get downhearted and don't let your trainee get depressed. Take at least half the responsibility for matching the wrong task to the person. If you decide jointly to withdraw an assignment, this is a crucial time to ask Barrie how she feels. What you hear may supply clues to more successful assignments in the future. Fortunately, you have an 80 percent chance of getting it right the first time. With each successful assignment your trainee will gain confidence, and you will gain the freedom to delegate work. You'll enhance value for your company and advance your own career.

The steps we just detailed actually read harder than they play. Consider a task you need to delegate soon, and try running it through the ten steps. Very quickly you will gain insight into the traps you must sidestep.

Good Delegation: From the Bottom Up

As you pored over the foregoing ten steps in delegating, you may have weighed the delegation skills of your own multiple bosses—noting which managers tend to delegate skillfully, and which of them tend to "dump" work on you, with all the attendant errors and omissions listed.

Multitask Challenges for Experienced Delegators

So far, this chapter has suggested hints for first-time delegators. But seasoned managers make many of the classic mistakes, too; mistakes from which you and your multiple managers must extricate yourselves. Successes follow when work is delegated with fairness and balance. Here's a case where that process still has miles to go.

Case 20. Overloaded and Boxed In

Presented by Aaron Zelachovsky, test engineer, manufacturing.

I've got two problems. One: Our boss tends to overload his best people (of whom I am one) because he knows we'll do things right. We're overworked. Weaker performers on the team, though willing, are untrained. They're bored, doing mostly "scut work." Two: When the neophytes turn to us stronger workmates for coaching, the boss gets in a lather; he thinks we're challenging his leadership in managing the team.

First Pass: Written Solutions From Seminar Colleagues

1. You strong people are your boss's lieutenants. If the boss won't train the new people, get yourselves assigned in some kind of rotation to help develop them, and get credit for it. Build some depth there.

2. You seem to have focused on only two levels: high achievers and weak performers. But in most teams, there are mid-level performers, too. These people are most often recruited to train the next talent level below them because they are closer to the learners in skill level, not superheroes.

3. To help bosses avoid concentrating work, chart current assignments against currently available skills and show where the work is concentrated on too few people. Show where training is needed to develop depth. Don't go head-to-head against your boss; let the wall chart do the talking.

4. What's all this trouble about concentrating work assignments? Don't let assignments be seen as rewards but simply as a matching of tasks with skills.

5. Around our shop, leaders spread the responsibility and the glory. The whole team works out up front where we need particular strengths and particular coverage. Then we suggest how to deploy the team's capabilities for providing that coverage. As a boss, I simply get the exercise started at our weekly meeting. The team staffs up the jobs and I OK them.

Your Reaction: What Advice Would You Endorse or Add?

_____

_____

_____

_____

_____

Second Thoughts Expressed in Group Discussion

Here's what evolved from group discussion of the written responses:

1. *You strong people can volunteer as trainer-developers.* Yes, and schedule a rational rotation for working and training. Get credit for both.

2. *Use mid-level achievers as trainers.* In discussion, teams agreed that highflyers may not care to slow down enough to train low achievers. Often, they demonstrate things with such speed and brilliance that learners get left in the dust. So 2's remarks about using "fellow humans" as trainers can be taken seriously. Performing tasks and training others are two distinct skill sets.

3. *Log assignments for fairness.* Probably not a nuisance if the log serves for follow-up, too.

4. *Don't let assignments be seen as rewards.* Teams got into heated discussion on this point. Most people saw good assignments as definite rewards, to be competed for and won. Able workers aspire to the "hot jobs," and develop a broad range of advanced skills for greater job security. So training newcomers in advanced skills is seen as an important contribution to the team, worthy of monetary rewards and recognition.

5. *Let the team staff up the projects.* Once again, seminar members from self-directed teams took this approach as

a natural. Seminar attendees from other types of companies found the idea intriguing but wondered, like Aaron, how they could encourage this without threatening the boss's power. They worried about bosses who do not yet grasp that sharing your power increases your power.

Consensus Recommendations

Getting good team coverage, deploying different talent levels across relevant types of work, and achieving a fair workload for all is a joint task for workers and their bosses. Whoever is worried (in this case an experienced worker) could sketch a chart showing current good workload matches and current workload misfires or shortfalls. Most reasonable bosses would say yes if invited to go over this with the team. A new modus operandi, with some team self-management, could result.

Tool Kit: Teamwork Distribution

Imagine your boss and worker team collaborating to redistribute the workload in an exciting situation: A great project arrives just when the team is fully loaded with urgent/important work. How will the team get the most valuable things done, using the most talent from every experience level? Your goals are achievement, fairness, and satisfaction. Figure 11 shows a tool to help you do it.

Working as a team, divide your current department load into risk categories: high-, mid-, and low-risk ranges. Team members handle those levels of risk for which they have training and experience. When a hot new assignment comes in, don't consider the whole thing high risk; don't reserve it for "star players" only. Instead, admit that the new task, once it becomes more familiar, will break down into levels that include: high, mid, and low risk.

So, from the start, divide the new task into varying risk levels and invite workers to participate at the level each can handle. Yes, the lion's share of the task may be done by your best workers, but participation (and its inherent development chances) can be spread more widely. Otherwise, you face the old situation that bothered Aaron. You load your best people with the new tasks, and dump their regular work on the people below—only to switch it back again when the prize assignment ends.

Dumping moves work downward onto the backs of lower-level people. But the high-mid-low risk method lets people move upward and across the workloads into the risk areas they can aspire to next.

Figure 11. New paradigm: teamwork distribution.

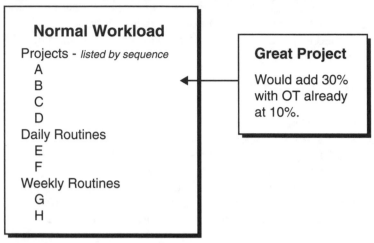

Normal Workload

Projects - *listed by sequence*
   A
   B
   C
   D
Daily Routines
   E
   F
Weekly Routines
   G
   H

Great Project

Would add 30%
with OT already
at 10%.

Load: 100% plus Overtime 10%

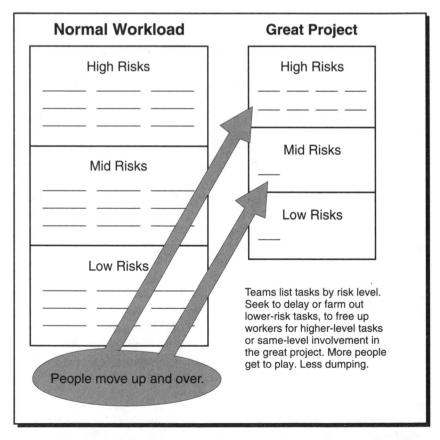

Normal Workload

High Risks

Mid Risks

Low Risks

Great Project

High Risks

Mid Risks

Low Risks

Teams list tasks by risk level.
Seek to delay or farm out
lower-risk tasks, to free up
workers for higher-level tasks
or same-level involvement in
the great project. More people
get to play. Less dumping.

People move up and over.

Learners get credit for trying harder; more experienced workers get credit for cross-training them. This new thinking—encouraging teamwork on setting up assignments—can produce the kind of inspired performance hikes seen in companies with self-managed teams.

Triumph or Tragedy: or Narrow Escape?

Delegation's path can be a thorny one, especially in your first attempt. Even for sophisticated supervisors, getting teams to assign and rotate themselves will require goodwill and maturity on the team's part, clear guidance from the team leader, and steadying support from the next higher level of management. All three crucial elements were missing in the case of Ellie F., a down-to-earth, easygoing office manager in her twenty-fifth year with a county facility in the southeast. She was promoted to head a department whose supervisor had just retired. She could see at once that discipline was lax. Despite rules requiring coverage of every office at that high-traffic hour, all the office ladies—as they had named themselves—took lunch together. They watched a daily soap opera in a TV lounge they had set up near the lunchroom. To start with, that program overran the official lunch break by twenty minutes. Ellie reminded the team of the coverage rule and insisted that, at the very least, they use a rotation system to provide lunchtime coverage for the public. She also required them to make up the twenty minutes by working earlier or later in the day. *"You have signed an agreement with the taxpayers,"* she reminded them, *"and it will go badly for us if they or your fellow county personnel notice this flouting of county rules."* So, the office ladies installed rotation and made up the time, but resentfully.

Soon, a new employee, Rima, arrived from another county facility to fill a vacancy in the department. The team quickly petitioned that she cover the daily lunch duty, leaving them free to gather as before. But Rima refused, disliking the late hour they had chosen for lunch, and citing a health condition that required her to eat earlier. Ellie sided with Rima in this, insisting that coverage be rotated by all as before, with Rima taking her turn. Though this new employee had arrived with good written reviews from her former bosses, it soon became clear that she was a problem. She slyly shirked hard work, came in late, used all of her sick days very quickly, could not be reached at the contact phone number she had provided, and generally skirted all rules. If nearby employees went out on assignment, she would quickly find that empty desk and make personal calls there until stopped. Rima had to be watched constantly. But her workmates, still angry with Ellie, encouraged Rima whenever she complained of her latest brush with Ellie over the rules. Ellie reacted promptly to each offense, providing oral and written reviews, doing retraining, or writing formal warnings as the situation required. Rima was courting dismissal.

Next, paperwork began disappearing. When Ellie would ask for work she had assigned to Rima, Rima would insist that she had already turned it in—that Ellie must have lost it. While clearing out a drawer in her own desk, Ellie found some of this missing work secreted there. She felt a chill as she understood Rima's intent to undermine. Now, when Ellie approached Rima, Rima would take out a notebook and start writing rapidly. She said it was to help her remember instructions. But her sly inflection made it clear that Rima, not Ellie, was now building a case. Ellie, as usual, informed her own supervisor about these difficulties. Unconcerned, he put her off, assuring her that things would settle down in time.

Feeling unsteady, Ellie made discreet inquiries of networking friends in Rima's former location. Some whispered that the "good reviews" had been given as an expedient to get rid of Rima without a fuss. When Ellie informed her boss of Rima's dubious background, he got testy, warning her against getting paranoid.

Within days, Ellie received official notice that Rima had made a formal complaint against her, charging harassment based on racial prejudice. No matter how much trust Ellie had earned in the past, her boss now doubted her. He cited lower morale among the "office ladies" who had been happy before—and now, these troubles with an employee whose former bosses had rated her "good." He wondered aloud whether Ellie had become too hard-nosed. She felt isolated as she awaited the official inquiry.

So she got busy. Humbly, she went to her previous manager, who had known her for years. (He happened to be of the same ethnic group as Rima.) *"Have you ever noticed any behavior or language of mine that could be construed as prejudiced?"* Ellie asked. *"No! of course not!"* the officer replied, genuinely shocked. He offered to testify on her behalf. She approached another friend in her network—the secretary to the Human Resources director—and she received further moral support there.

Ellie handled herself well before the committee, whereas Rima contradicted herself on several points and could not defend her lateness and absenteeism record. The committee exonerated Ellie, but to her dismay, they left Rima in place, with only a caution. Ellie's peace of mind was shaken. Despite the pile-up of work, she took a week's vacation that was due her, and networked some more.

The senior manager in whom Ellie had confided now invited her to head one of his departments. She accepted at once.

Meanwhile, Rima—now totally unsupervised—escalated to bigger things. A security officer observed her putting county property into her car. Security pursued the matter and she was soon fired. One of the office ladies took over as supervisor of the department. The soap-opera lunches were immediately restored.

"But that," says Ellie, now heading a healthy department, *"is someone else's concern."* As you ponder this case, you may feel as if all these people were trapped in a time warp, thirty years back. Yet, it should convince you that your delegating success, even if you are experienced, will require:

- Reasonable goodwill and maturity in the people to whom you assign work, especially if they want team power.
- Clear guidance from you as team leader, with joint, graphic task planning open to the whole team.
- Occasional coaching from the level above you if you run into difficulties while delegating work.
- Support from your network to help you keep your balance.

Summary: The Delicate Art of Delegating

1. *Overcome your fear of delegating; you can still control quality.*

2. *It would be "quicker to do it yourself" only once.*

3. *Choose repetitive, well-formatted tasks to delegate to volunteers, retirees, or college or high school students.*

4. *Don't let confidentiality bar you; simply code or protect sensitive data.*

5. *Release work on a gradient: easiest first.*

6. *Estimate learning time, not just performance time.*

7. *Review these ten steps before delegating:*

- Write up task: Focus on steps and skills.
- Build in controls on quantity, quality, budget.
- Select the right person based on skills and enthusiasm.
- Make the job attractive: Show opportunities, rewards.
- Teach the job step by step; demonstrate.
- Allow two-way feedback: Use open questions.
- Revise and reset goals for learning as well as performance.
- Monitor, don't stifle; both sides agree on critical points.
- Give operating support. Go public.
- Reward effort. Public praise, private correction. (Willingly reassign in case of task mismatch.)

8. *See work as a reward, not a burden. Let people compete for great assignments.*

9. *Teach teams to deploy themselves across tasks with high-, mid-, and low-risk assignments. Let them use wall charts to clarify.*

10. *Use your network, not just your boss, to help you solve delegation dilemmas.*

8 Dealing With Difficult Bosses

F rustrated employees love to complain about their bosses. Once they attain maturity themselves, they often look back with regret on the harsh judgments they applied to the bosses of their youth. When I poll competent managers, most agree that at least 80 percent of bosses are smart, sane, and decent. Then there are the 10 percent of charismatic, larger-than-life bosses—often operating at genius levels—who can make you feel lucky to be on the same planet with them.

Finally, there are the 10 percent of bosses who should have a bull's-eye painted on their backsides, but this baffling minority seem to have been born boot-proof. Some are simply amoral—or else so self-involved—that they scarcely note the existence of lower mortals, much less other people's feelings. These sociopaths cannot be sensitized by veiled warnings or mild suggestions from others. When they are finally (and too often, reluctantly) chastised by their senior managers, they express innocent amazement. Dealing with a toxic boss can be exhausting enough in itself, but add it to your multi-boss pressures, and your bafflement comes to the boil. The flip side of Pareto's Law suggests that your "tiny toxic percent" of demand will cause 80 percent of your agony at work.

Your Difficult Bosses: Toxic or Just Tough?

Generally, people are too discreet to speak ill of their problem bosses in seminars; they tend to do it privately, over coffee or drinks with a couple of after-hours buddies, or they catch the speaker alone at a break. A lot of help is exchanged in these chats. Here's a case in point:

Case 21. New Boss Nukes All

Presented by Olivia Hanks, publications manager at an East Coast university.

Among my bosses are four college presidents and four alumni directors who make many demands on our staff. But I report directly to a newly hired division head—a young striver who volunteers our unit for huge tasks without regard to who will do the extra work and how. Out of the blue, she convinced the university that the public information group could be let go— that we could easily take on their work. Now, she commands: *"Just get it done."* She ignores our reasoned requests for low-cost help, then repudiates us when senior managers complain of defaults. She calls us "wimps" to our faces in staff meetings, which have become torture. *"It's your job to convince me if I'm wrong,"* she challenges. But we've felt the lash of her caustic wit, along with her distortions. Top management loves her cost cuts, unaware of the chaos inside the department.

I used to be famously gutsy but, as the senior person reporting to her, I am loath to commit "job-icide" by going over her head to complain, when I'm only four years from retirement.

First Pass: Solutions From Her Hallway Companions

1. Four years is a long time to be miserable. Try to transfer.

2. You could foot-drag on the plans of this "hotshot," but don't do it solo. If all of you join forces, management may wise up.

3. When she imposes huge new workloads on you all, map out a team proposal for *compliance.* Head up some charts: "How to Handle a 100% Work Hike" or "How to Heft a 300% Workload." Show various routes, risks, and trade-offs. Show it like it is, but present yourselves as problem-solvers, not resisters. Get this striving boss to dig into the HOW, not the WHETHER, of handling these workloads.

4. Document. If all of you take notes in those meetings where she uses name-calling, your group testimony may hold water. Assign roles: debater, data-gatherer, networker, or peacemaker. Let team members choose various jobs in negotiating a better situation. Take it up in writing with Miss Hotshot first; then take it higher.

5. What if management hired her to "clean house" in your unit? Can you get data on how well your output stacks up against that of other university publication groups? There must be an association that can tell you what kind of load is typical. This lady may be acting out of ignorance . . . or superior knowledge!

Your Reaction: What Advice Would You Endorse or Add?

_____

_____

_____

_____

_____

Second Thoughts Expressed in Group Discussion

1. *Transfer.* Careful: If publishing is all you do, and all publications are under this one roof, you might not be able to transfer.

2. *Joint foot-dragging might bring on more abuse at first.* Admit this risk.

3. *Map out the increased workload size.* Not only should you post those charts on the wall, you should memo or e-mail this boss that you have produced some alternative plans for lifting these huge loads, and you need her approval, budget OK, or consultation—because such plans would have to be radical. She would not dare ignore such a written invitation. Once she starts talking, you can all take notes or use a recorder (with her consent) "to capture everyone's ideas." Maybe she'll run a better meeting when she knows it can be scrutinized later.

4. *Document the meeting; take different roles.* Yes. You're more likely to improve things by changing your own behaviors than by attacking hers. By dividing responsibilities for various aspects of problem solving, you stand a better chance of producing a meeting result. Document—not to trap her—but to follow through on your own proposed solutions.

5. *Is she a hired assassin?* The one good thing is—with the adjoining department gone—the university probably cannot meet its publication deadlines without you. So you may be in a stronger position than you think. Definitely research how you stack up against other university publication groups. And, since your institution is in a cost-cutting mode, highlight your willingness to improve operations at lowest cost.

Consensus Recommendations

You may find it amazing that a whole group of educated people can be cowed by one unmannerly newcomer. But when her first act is to "nuke" the department next door, survivors tend to hesitate. Was she hired to drop a bomb that management had already fashioned? By networking, you might find out. If she's acting as a free agent, you might persuade someone powerful to restrain her, but you'll do better if you focus on solutions to the university's production and cost problems. Sell solutions, not complaints.

Object Lessons in Arbitrary Demands

Bear in mind what nasty outcomes can ensue when impossible goals are announced with a "just do it" mandate. Two cases in point:

About five years ago, salespeople for an old, established information service were told to capture 10 percent more business in one year. They already owned more than 90 percent of the market. Some desperate or unscrupulous salespeople could see a quick route: Move current industrial customers to higher service levels than they actually needed. Because customers could not access the data to gauge whether they needed to rise a level, they accepted the salesmen's warnings to buy the increased service now, before prices could go up. An internal manager blew the whistle, but the information company dawdled. Only when the story leaked onto page one of *The New York Times*'s business section did the company halt the practice. Some customers sued for reparations; others were offered "free" services in the months that followed. It's amazing how many customers forgave, but few competitors offered these services at the time.

Shortly thereafter, a famous retailer shredded years of hard-earned reputation the same way. It ordered its auto repair managers to increase sales by a large percentage, without new promotional or technical advances to make it happen. Desperate managers began "finding" auto defects that needed repairs. Again, a whistle-blower began a train of events that brought about reform, but not before the courts levied fines on the company. Trust was dissolved between management and employees and between the company and its clientele. It may take years of fresh effort to restore the company's good reputation.

An Illuminating Interview: Dealing With Anger

Mark Ruffino, a financial analyst, shared this experience during an after-hours session.

My boss is a real Caligula. But he's brilliant when it comes to investments. Our board hangs on his every word. He asked

me to stay one night (when I was already exhausted) to produce figures for a sudden late dinner meeting with the brass.
I objected, warning him that we could not come up with accurate data in time. He gave me that "death look" of his, so
I stayed and did my best. He went into the meeting.

It took me an hour or so to clear up the debris from this job.
Just as I was leaving, he emerged. He came straight over to
my cube and started to scream. He slammed down the report we had put together and yelled: *"How could you be so
stupid??? Can't you see these calculations are completely off?
Do I have to do everything myself???"*

He went on and on until my eyes glazed over. I just let him
rant. I could see some of the brass staring at us from the
hallway behind him. I stood up, and said quite loudly but
firmly:

*"Boss, I take this very seriously, of course. I did warn you of
the dangers involved. Now excuse me while I go see what I
can do to repair it."*

I brushed past him, walked quietly out of the building and
drove home, shaking with rage. I don't know if he stood there
half the night waiting for me to return from wherever I went
to "repair it," but I knew that was the right thing to do.

The next morning, I sent him an e-mail asking if he needed
me to send revised figures to the meeting members. He
e-mailed back a single word: *"Yes."* I did the numbers, I sent
them out; that's the last I heard of it.

Mark's listeners were wowed by this tactic, but some declared
they would flinch at leaving the presence of a boss while under siege.
Many psychologists advise, however, that you'd be wiser to "remove
the target" when an abusive person starts firing large-caliber verbal
pellets. This saves the attacker from escalating to verbal "manslaugh-
ter"; it spares you from hollering over the roar of another's rage. It
preserves your dignity.
Bear in mind those vital opening words Mark used:

"Boss, I take this very seriously."

This sounds respectful without being apologetic. Remember his final
comment, too: He focused on *"repairs"* . . . moving the boss away
from the error and on toward solutions. By using these tactics, he kept

his dignity and saved the boss from further embarrassment in front of senior eavesdroppers.

Tool Kit: A Five-Step Strategy for Dealing With Angry Bosses

Some listeners confessed that they had been "chewed out" by bosses in the presence of others. Here's what they recommended.

1. Break off. Get away briefly.

2. Fix the error if possible.

3. As soon as you are calm, check to see if the "screamer" is also calm. Don't wait a day or two. Bosses may think they got away with it, and they hate to be reminded.

4. Get privacy. Then open with a report on the error:

"Boss, I apologize for the error. I've made the correction and sent it."

If possible, state any plan you have for making up or curtailing the costs.

5. Move on to repair the interpersonal process. Do it in steps:

"Boss, my intention is always to do my best for the company. I want our relationship to improve, not decline, so I have a request: I feel embarrassed whenever I am critiqued in front of others. If I should ever make a mistake again, I'm asking for privacy while we discuss it."

Notice that the pronoun *I* is used throughout. The pronoun *you* is strictly avoided. This method is crafted to elicit the least guilt or blame and to leave your attacker a face-saving way to do what you ask. Does it guarantee a peaceful accord? No. The other guy is still free to stay angry. But does it guarantee that you make a peaceful approach? Yes. It lets you do your half of the transaction in a civil, non-blaming way.

Even if you feel homicidal after an outburst from your boss, convince yourself that improving your relationship is a sensible goal in your own interest. That will help you avoid the sarcasm you might fervently wish to express. Rehearse your five-point response until you sound like your heart is in it.

Then say your lines and go home.

Coping With Harassers or Abusers

Though American case law has been building for several years, there are still no easy answers when one person accuses another—even when further witnesses corroborate your complaint. High legal fees and a tortuous process tend to scare off many justified complainers. That's why we recommend immediate, unequivocal self-help as a first step.

Case 22. A Code of Honor

The assistant to the CEO of a global oil company shared this with me confidentially. The location and details have been masked.

Like many companies in our region, we move the local presidents around every three years or so. In my long career, I have been assistant to many wonderful managers from every part of the world. I've been well-educated and consider myself sophisticated, but I was alarmed by the behavior of a new president, a European here for several months without his wife and family. His demands on me became overly dependent; he intruded on my weekends, leaning on me to handle his personal and financial affairs.

Finally, he started pressuring me to go out with him for evening dates. When I said no, he confided that he was obsessed with me. In our culture, this kind of pressure is deeply offensive.

Soon, at a company dinner, his whispered remarks to me were particularly bad. I started to leave abruptly, and encountered one of my former bosses in the hallway. He's a local man—now vice chairman of the company. I was so upset, I could not hide my distress; he knows me quite well. We stepped into an anteroom and he asked me what was the matter. As discreetly as I could, I told him of this pressure from the new president. I feared greatly to tell him, but I felt obliged to. Here's what he said:

> Thank you for telling me. You did right. Now, I want you to go home and forget all about this. You will never see this behavior repeated. I will take care of it.

Whatever he did or said later, I don't know, but his assurances proved true. Though he has never alluded to the past, this president is now the soul of respect, courtesy, and proper behavior to me.

Conclusion

This assistant's confidants were reluctant to add anything. They marveled that despite all the brouhaha over the difficulty of controlling aberrant behavior, there are still places in the world where the top people know exactly how to act *subrosa* to end such behavior. All agreed that this secretary was smart to speak up to a person of power and honor in her culture. Because she had earned impeccable credibility with a long succession of bosses, she could now call on it. By speaking to the vice chairman, she removed the one protection that her abuser needed—secrecy.

Tool Kit: A Subtle Defense Network

Before harassment laws came into play (and since they have proved unevenly difficult to apply) people in some American organizations have created their own subtle ways to deal with predators. Here is one:

In a certain university, women first got together in support groups to make quality or productivity gains, or to get fair compensation in hard-to-measure activities like administration.

But they quickly found ways to help each other with difficult matters of discrimination and abuse. In one department where I consulted for several months, the women had worked out a simple and powerful weapon against abusers. This was their *modus operandi:*

In rebuffing an ambiguous first offense by a groper or harasser, women taught each other to say: *"That behavior is unacceptable"* or *"The answer is no."*

Their next sentence was crucial:

"I will take this first instance as a mistake on your part. Be warned: Any further approach you make will be seen as a deliberate offense." Then, they would continue:

"I belong to a women's support network, and we have agreed to report any such behavior on the second occurrence. If you want to be blacklisted by all the women in this institution, you are on notice. Be aware . . . just as you keep your activities secret, so do we. You can protect your privacy and prevent further action by stopping this behavior now."

Then, the woman would get up and walk away.

These women meant what they said. One executive, old enough

to know better, persisted after a first warning. His victim, a new employee, seemed young and naïve. But she was in the network. Once she reported the second incident (which several of the women knew to be plausible), the women in the support group went into subtle action. Any time the predator would approach any of the women— even on appropriate business—the women would take a step back or move abruptly away to reply from a distance. They did this even if he passed them in a hallway. As he approached, they all stepped quickly aside without smiling or making eye contact. A single day of this body language spoke volumes to any observer.

Experiencing this action, even once, was enough to curtail unwanted behavior. No woman has needed to start a lawsuit over this man.

There are many companies with well-publicized programs that protect people from harassers. But the all-out legal path has looked pretty exhausting, both emotionally and financially, for victims. A few whistle-blowers, courageous and righteously indignant, continue to break trail for others to follow.

On a milder note, an engineer for a Dutch firm was quite forthright with a boss who used disrespectful terms when speaking about her to outsiders. He seemed oblivious to the offense he was giving. She found a private moment to feed back to him how his remarks offended her. He was surprised, but he began to see how his language might be taken as offensive. She accepted that he'd been honestly unaware, and offered to "signal" him if he should err again. They agreed on a completely neutral code word she could use. Once she began signaling, he understood and checked his behavior immediately. They shared more than one knowing grin about it in the weeks that followed. The problem dissolved and their trust deepened.

With apparent harassers or abusers, state your objections immediately so there can be no doubt of your attitude. Document from the first. If behavior continues, follow your company's procedures: Report the offense to the designated authority. Even if you don't have the support of a women's network yet, warn the offender that you do—so the weapon of secrecy is denied him. Then, get busy joining a women's support network!

Luckily, intentional predators are rare. But moody bosses are plentiful. When added to your multi-boss demands, one person's moody antics can take a toll.

Case 23. The Moody Manager

Presented, after hours, by Harold Kohn, software product development manager

One of my bosses is so moody, I swear he should be on lithium. We can be right on Monday, wrong on Tuesday for the same actions. We work in a very demanding setting. Sometimes he'll defend us upstairs, other times he'll hang us out to dry, or flame us via e-mail for all to see. We've learned to duck when he gets calls from his ex-wife, or when he gets reamed by his own boss. But his highs grow fewer and his lows seem to hit closer together.

First Pass: Solutions From After-Hours Colleagues

1. Notice his patterns and make yourselves scarce at those times.

2. Note and prevent whatever sets him off: inaccuracy, omissions, lateness, or bad news. You could either team up to head off selected problems, or else "rotate the duty" so no one person has to be the bearer of all bad news.

3. The guy may be sick, just as you suspect. If you were sick, would you hope for understanding? Maybe you could cut him a little slack. Work at not taking outbursts personally. You could say:

"I react better to requests than to criticism, so what is your request here, Mike?"

Rehearse and use it repeatedly.

or say: "I agree that this is important. Here's what you're asking me to do now . . ." then, review the bidding so he doesn't stay agitated, and so you get some clarity on instructions.

4. Document these outbursts. Then show him the pattern. If he won't concur, then you could seek confidential advice from Human Resources, expressing your concern about his health or department morale.

5. You could ask him to chat with Human Resources, or suggest that he consult with the corporate Employee Assistance Program if he is facing any personal issues that are none of your business. Sure, he'll probably get mad, but you need to get off the dime when outbursts start escalating. If you want to confide about personal pressures you have faced, he may feel your sincerity. That's up to you.

Your Reaction: What Advice Would You Endorse or Add?

_____

_____

_____

Second Thoughts Expressed in Group Discussion

1. *Notice patterns: make yourself scarce.* Conversely, express empathy. Ask if there is anything you can do to make the business day go better.

2. *Head off irritations if you can.* This kindness makes sense if you don't have to do it too often. With repeat incidents, work might grind to a halt.

3. *Understand. Ask for what you need to get work done.* Yes: Making this your automatic, detached response would reduce your stress.

4. *Document, show a pattern: seek Human Resources advice for yourself.* The correct escalation if you fail at 1, 2, and 3.

5. *Suggest he seek help; confide so he sees you identify with him.* Taking such a personal risk would be a friendly gift, not an obligation. If you take this risk, harbor no expectations about the outcome.

A Corroborating Account: One executive assistant related this incident about her former boss, a high-ranking military officer. As he came under more and more stress from an advancing illness, he isolated more and produced less. As his birthday approached, he warned that he did not want the usual cake and trimmings that were customary in that office. The team, thinking he needed cheering up, overrode the secretary's advice to "cool it."

When the staff approached singing "Happy Birthday," the officer starting shouting: he lunged for the cake and stabbed the pen he was holding right into the center of the cake, splashing himself and others with icing and lighted candles. He stormed off into his office, leaving the whole room speechless. After years of cracking jokes about "the men in the white coats," this assistant had the sad task of calling them for her boss.

Consensus Recommendations

Onlookers agreed that even the strongest people among us are vulnerable to illness or overload. All agreed that "doing unto others as you'd want done unto you" is a good, general approach, as long as you curtail your expectations.

Caution: Bosses Are Human

Case 24. Looking Out for Number One

Related by Claire Pearson, budget analyst for a large R&D firm.

After our most recent round of layoffs, I got fed up with the gallows atmosphere and considered a job offer from a friendly vendor. When I told my boss about the offer, he talked me out of it, assuring me that our company would soon stabilize, that he needed me with him for the large challenges we now faced as a team. He got me a modest bonus immediately, and promised to fight for a raise and promotion soon. So I've stayed, working a murderous schedule out of loyalty and hope. Guess what? My boss just took a great job in another company, which must have been in the works all along. That snake used me to clear up his backlog and buy him a graceful exit. On top of it, he parted with the news that "we got shot down" on my raise and promotion.

Midway through Claire's story, her hallway companions had already sensed the outcome. Her boss had simply looked out for himself first; he had fed her convenient half-truths, using the bonus as a sop to his conscience. Claire had learned this much: that we should never require other people to put our interests ahead of theirs as the last lifeboat loads up! It could happen, of course, but we should not expect it.

Consensus Recommendations

In the future, Claire will make career decisions based on what is best for her. Then she will do what she can, realistically, to leave her old employer in good operating shape when she moves on. But personal sacrifice is not required of any of us in order to qualify as a team player. What factors are required? The hallway group explored that next.

Getting Along: The Gory Glory of Teamwork

How do people know that you, your bosses, and your colleagues are a team? The most noticeable thing about teams (as opposed to individuals who sit in the same area or report to the same boss) is that team members spend time together, solve problems together, create results together . . . and, in the process, they develop ease with one another, blending their diverse strengths, temperaments, work habits, and needs. Through continuous interactions, they help bolster one another's confidence, even while admitting awareness of one another's shortcomings.

If your team has begun to crumble—if harmony has slipped—you may have fallen unwittingly into a trap: **heedless patterns of interacting.** Like family members taking one another for granted, you may neglect the courtesies you would extend to strangers; you may let familiarity breed contempt. Just as in families, people rely more on nonverbal than verbal communication, people in teams can begin to communicate by looks, gestures and silences—subliminal, emotion-based actions. You may sink to using sarcasm, mean jokes, or little acts of sabotage rather than simple, open requests.

People who feel slighted may retaliate subtly for real or fancied insults: They may "forget" vital requests, or mutter or complain in rest rooms or parking lots. They may whine, criticize, or speculate about the motives of other team members. Hurt people may retaliate by quietly delaying or blocking results. Because team members know each other's vulnerabilities, they can deal tough body blows once they cross the line from ally to adversary. As trust erodes, the team structure can grow hollow by degrees, crumbling under small, new pressures without warning. During periods of intense effort, team members must remind themselves to observe the courtesies of life with special attention.

Restore Courtesy: Repair Harmony

If you notice any toxic behavior pattern forming between you and a boss or team member, choose a day when you all feel reasonable and rested, and then open it up. In the clearest and warmest manner you can muster, get it across that:

1. You feel uncomfortable with the current state of affairs and want to restore harmony.
2. You have some brief, concrete ideas about ways YOU can change, and would welcome the other person's ideas.
3. You want to know what you can both do now to help team harmony, get what you need, and restore your balance.

Don't expect miracles; it takes time and persistence to overcome a toxic pattern even if it's fairly fresh. But do begin. Clear the air while irritations and doubts are still minor.

The Cure Begins With You

In a toxic situation, you may think, I'm the one who has been offended. Why should I make the first move? If you're wondering who should make the first overture, here's the answer: the one who can.

Triumphs and Turnarounds: Closing the Lion's Den

Some managements opt to tolerate baffling behavior, applying slight "course corrections" while allowing the "bad guys" to stay in place. They are especially tempted to tolerate a difficult person who can contribute unique values to the enterprise. This practice may frustrate naïve people seeking perfect justice or sweet revenge, but you'd do well to learn peaceful coexistence with it.

A few years ago, I did a time management course for a paint and polymer manufacturer based in Britain. The audience was to be Research & Development managers and researchers, along with the twenty secretaries and text editors who prepared their technical proposals.

Their proposals, as much as their polymers, were the heart of the company's business. As always, I asked the organizer whether there were any special problems, changes, or challenges I should know about. *"Nothing special . . . we're just heading into a period of great R&D expansion and we want to be ready,"* was his encouraging reply. When I arrived at the site, the president and his secretary, a mature and pleasant woman named Felicia, whisked me into the executive suite for morning coffee.

Only then did the president tell me of his hidden agenda for the day: He wanted to force the Research & Development director—a brilliant researcher but a hopelessly abrasive personality—to improve relationships with his staffers, particularly with the twenty secretary-editors who had grown to hate him. His fellow scientists were not fond of "Clive" either, but he gave them the assignments they wanted and the credit they needed—and they considered him a genius. With the women, Clive's behavior was pointedly different: He gave off impatience and contempt whenever they approached him. Except for this training session, all attempts to get this man into a room with the secretaries had failed. Naturally, I did not like being a party to an entrapment. But the president was both clever and kind, and he promised to redirect any explosive encounter to good ends. "It's your company," I thought, and we negotiated details to go ahead. The morning was tense enough, but the final afternoon session—I had held the topic of conflict to the end—looked perilous.

When a secretary-editor complained discreetly that the text production team needed earlier warning and clearer rationales for handling priority changes, Clive exploded. *"Why would I share information with a bunch of silly secretaries like you who spend your time examining your split ends?"* He rose to leave the room, but the president stopped him.

Clive, please sit down. I want to thank you for finally letting us hear your perceptions about the support team. I do not share your attitude; on the contrary, I believe you are blind to the capabilities of anyone outside your own technology. Changing your attitude will be a slow business. And we *will* embark on it. Meanwhile, by going public in this way, you make it impossible to work alongside these women. So let us all try something different.

The president paused to let this sink in.

Because we value your brilliance at polymer applications, I am offering you a chance to retreat behind closed doors in your lab. I propose that when liaison is needed with the production team, my assistant, Felicia, will act as clearinghouse for the team's questions and needs. She will direct the secretary-editors in the unit. Felicia and I have discussed this possibility, and she is willing. She has also discussed it with the secretarial group, and they are willing.

Now it's up to you, Clive, whether *you* are willing. In a few minutes, I'd like us all to regroup here. You'll tell us whether this proposal will suit you, or whether we need to create a counterproposal.

Clive, standing again said:

No need to wait. This proposal will suit me admirably.

The man clearly meant it. He walked out of the room. Faces were jubilant, but there were no "high fives"—no applause. This was England. We went on with the rest of the seminar.

When I checked weeks later, I learned that both the working atmosphere and the group's productivity had risen even more than expected. Since then, I've seen many cases where wise managers focused their resident geniuses on the narrow specialties in which they had skill, and spared the rest of the company from dealings in the lion's den.

Conclusion. With enough detachment, goodwill, and help from powerful senior managers, most of your dealings with difficult people can be made easier. The important thing is for you to begin as you mean to go on—without intense reaction, without taking offense, with as much detachment and objective pursuit of options as you can muster. Light up that motto in neon just behind your eyes: *Other people's behavior is mostly about them. . . . and save yourself a lot of stress.*

Summary: Getting Along With Difficult Bosses (and Others)

1. *When overwhelmed by a hotshot boss, map out options as a team.* Involve the boss in the search for *how,* to illuminate problems with *whether.*

2. *Document repetitive verbal abuse; warn about toxic patterns.*

3. *Get comparative data on load sizes handled by similar departments serving multiple bosses.* Professional groups can often help with this.

4. *If you are a boss yourself, never command "just do it" when assigning difficult goals.* If you are a subordinate receiving such an order, get an OK on your action outline. (This allows a hasty boss to retreat.) Jointly create behavioral guidelines that are legally and morally acceptable.

5. *During any boss's tirade, express respect; say you take this seriously.* Then escape the target zone while offering to fix it or to regroup.

6. *Fix the error.* Then, in privacy, seek to mend the relationship.

7. *If accosted by a harasser, say a flat no.* Warn mild or ambiguous accosters that a second offense will not be kept secret. Leave the scene. Document. Be prepared to report serious first offenses and all second offenses to a trustworthy officer or to a support group.

8. *See excessive moodiness as a sign of possible illness; this helps you to remain detached and merciful.*

9. *Ask moody people to use the type of communication you prefer: descriptive or requesting, rather than judging or blaming.*

10. *Create a signaling system to help people see and stop toxic patterns.*

11. *With teammates, observe the courtesies.* Don't take each other for granted.

12. *When feeling hurt, carefully review your expectations of others.*

13. *The cure begins with you.* Who should mend fences? The one who can!

Afterword

Some Final Suggestions

You've Seen Some Solutions

Throughout most of this book, I've focused on solving the problems that you face in juggling multiple demands. Cases and stories gave you vivid evidence that you are not alone in your struggle with priorities, overloads, deadlines, and time and personality pressures. The testimony of others offered you many new tools and options for handling your next challenges. Check the summaries at the close of each chapter for techniques that will work for you.

Don't Ignore the Advantages in Multi-Boss Jobs

Remember, there's an upside to the multi-boss environment. While you face big challenges, you also get startling advantages from working with multiple bosses. In fact, our survey respondents praised some of the gains they have made from working with multiple bosses:

- Wider exposure to information, strategies, and tactics in a host of business applications.
- Deeper experience with varied management styles. Many ways to think, negotiate, and solve problems. (There's no *one* best way.)
- Direct mentoring from important executives. "Face time" with more leaders, which can broaden your power base.
- More task variety, less boredom, and faster-paced days.
- Added allies. When you make a mistake or lose favor with one boss, you can still get approval from the others.
- Greater promotability: More chances to "show your stuff"—you glide in the slipstream of people who are climbing fast.
- Greater job security. In a reorganization, some bosses will leave; others will survive and keep you with them. In fact, some who leave will invite you to join them in their new companies.

- Just as in sales, it can take thirty calls to land one order—so in your career it can take thirty bosses to position you for one glorious career chance.

Trigger the Instinct to Negotiate

As you've seen in each chapter, managers, technologists, and administrative assistants use negotiation, time after time, to solve legitimate priority conflicts. Whatever negotiating skills you've been exposed to, you must first concentrate on building the *instinct to negotiate* every time you feel pressured. Perhaps the Five-A's method can help you awaken that instinct:

1. *Accept.* Acknowledge that other people's behavior is mostly about them. See each agreement as a tapestry you weave together, with a constantly evolving design based on a constantly maturing trust.

2. *Ask.* If there's anything you don't fathom about any boss's needs, it is simpler to ask; don't assume or ascribe motives.

3. *Affirm.* Willingly acknowledge and express your own needs and invite your multiple bosses to do the same.

4. *Act.* Readily make an offer or propose a fresh option. No negotiation is cut in stone: Rewrite a contract anytime, especially if new advantages appear.

5. *Advance.* Don't be drawn into toxic complaints or disputes about the past. Focus on what is needed now. Consistently move the action forward to what is still possible.

Flex Your Negotiating Skills

Keep this next list handy. Before you start negotiating with conflicting bosses, quickly scan these steps to avoid mishaps. You'll become a stronger and more supple negotiator the more often you remember to exercise your skills.

Ten Steps for Solving Serious Conflicts

1. *Make negotiation visible.* Outline your risks and needs on an index card. Let the other party see the card. Invite them to do a risks-needs list of their own.

2. *Keep things simple.* Settle one issue at a time . . . not all the issues of life.

3. *Keep your tone respectful.* Open with appreciation for time allotted and courtesies extended.

4. *Keep talk open.* No mysteries, no ambushes, no blaming.

5. *Listen carefully.* Hear a complaint as a need to be met. Thank the other person for clarifying an issue to be solved.

6. *When multiple bosses clash, do not focus on "who is right" but go for "what will work" . . . seek outcomes that reduce risk.*

7. *Keep the climate cool.* Don't push for agreement if the other party is surprised, angry, or tired. Suggest a time-out, no matter how rushed you all feel.

8. *In any negotiation, post a little sign for yourself where only you can see it:*

WHAT AM I DOING TO MAKE IT EASIER FOR THE OTHER PERSON TO SAY YES?

---

9. *When you reach agreement, thank your bosses for working with you toward a solution.*

10. *Celebrate specific savings or successes achieved through negotiating.* Make your bosses feel as good about it as you do.

Decide Whom You Should Manage

This book is titled *Managing Multiple Bosses.* That's what audience members keep asking us to show them. But you are now aware of the ironic truth: Whatever tools and techniques you use, you can manage only yourself.

As you embark on the next phase of your life with multi-boss teams, combine your negotiating instincts and skills to increase team clarity, unity, grace, and flow. The extra support you get and give one another will lift you toward new solutions, new successes, and new career security, whatever happens to your job.

More power to you all!

Index